Machine-Gun Squadron

Machine-Gun Squadron

The 20th Machine Gunners from
British Yeomanry Regiments in the
Middle East Campaign of
the First World War

A. M. G.

LEONAUR

Machine-Gun Squadron: The 20th Machine Gunners from British Yeomanry Regiments in the Middle East Campaign of the First World War
by A. M. G.

Originally published under the title:

Through Palestine with the Twentieth Machine-Gun Squadron

Published by Leonaur Ltd

ISBN: 978-1-84677-160-6 (hardcover)
ISBN: 978-1-84677-155-2 (softcover)

http://www.leonaur.com

Publisher's Notes

In the interests of authenticity, the spellings, grammar and place names used have been retained from the original editions.

The opinions of the authors represent a view of events in which he was a participant related from his own perspective, as such the text is relevant as an historical document.

The views expressed in this book are not necessarily those of the publisher.

Contents

Foreword

This book has been compiled with the object of enabling the members of the 20th Machine-Gun Squadron to recall the principal incidents in its history, as well as to allow their friends and relations to obtain some idea of their experiences whilst they were serving with the Egyptian Expeditionary Force.

Although no pains have been spared to obtain accuracy, the statements made must, necessarily, not be regarded as absolutely authoritative.

Beyond doubt, many brave deeds, fully deserving of mention in these pages, must have been unavoidably overlooked, in which case the leniency of readers is requested.

In view of the probability that the incidents described herein may be read by many persons who have not been to the East, explanations have frequently been included, which might appear to some as unnecessary.

The writer is indebted to several members of the Squadron for their valuable assistance, without which, obviously, it would have been very difficult to have given an adequate account of any particular incident at which he was not present in person.

The Author
1st July 1920

Glossary

The following are a few descriptive terms which occur in the following pages, with place-names, and the abbreviations used.

ABU: Father

AIN: Spring

BEIT: House

BIRKETT: Pool

BIR: Well

DEIR: Monastery

ED, EL, ER, ES, EZ The definite article THE

JEBEL: Mountain

JISR: Bridge

KEFR: Village

KAHN: Inn

KHURBET (abbrev. KH.): Ruin

MAKHADET: Ford

NAHR: River

NEBY: A Prophet

RAS: Head, cape, top

SHEIKH (abbrev. SH.): Chief, elder, saint

TEL: Mound (especially one covering ruins)

WADI: A dry watercourse

Time

The following table shows the military method of stating the time which is used throughout this book:

1 a.m.	01.00	2.35 p.m.	14.35
2 a.m.	02.00	3.50 p.m.	15.50
3.15 a.m.	03.15	8 p.m.	20.00
6.45 a.m.	06.45	10 p.m.	22.00
12 midday	12.00	12 midnight	24.00
1 p.m.	13.00	12.15 a.m.	00.15

CHAPTER 1

Formation of the Squadron

It was on the 4th July 1917 that authority was given to the 7th Mounted Brigade (then at Ferry-Post, Ismailia), for the formation of a Machine-Gun Squadron to be known as the "20th." It was to consist of "Headquarters" and only three sub-sections, there being but two regiments (instead of the usual three) in the 7th Brigade.

On July 4th, Lieut. E.P. Cazalet and Lieut. E.B. Hibbert, machine gun officers of the Notts (Sherwood Rangers) Yeomanry and South Notts Hussars respectively, brought their sub-sections to the new camp. Lieut. C.D. Macmillan also arrived from the "S.N.H." From these two regiments there came, in all, 3 officers, 121 men and 98 animals (horses and mules). The "A" Sub-section was formed of "S.R.Y." men; the "B" Sub-section of "S.N.H." men, "C" Sub-section being composed of both "S.R.Y." and "S.N.H." men.

From the commencement, the Squadron "carried on" under very difficult conditions, as, out of its total strength of 121, only 30 men were qualified gunners, and 63 had never previously been attached to a Machine Gun Section. Then there were fresh animals to draw from "Remounts" besides new saddlery and equipment from "Ordnance". The health of the Squadron, also, was at first none too good; a large number of men had contracted malaria whilst with the Brigade in Salonica, and many others were liable to septic sores, after two years' sojourn in Egypt, Suvla and Salonica. From time to time, seven days' leave was granted to small parties to the Rest Camp, Port Said, and lucky were those men whose turn it was to go!

In due course, on July 30th 1917, Lieut. D. Marshall (Fife & Forfar Yeomanry), arrived from the 4th "M.G." Company. He had been "posted" as Commanding Officer, and "took over" from Lieut. Cazalet; shortly afterwards he was promoted to the rank of Captain.

The first reinforcements to reach the Squadron from the training centre at Maresfield Park, England, were Ptes. Ramsay and Wick on August 4th 1917. Pte. Ramsay at once took up the duties of orderly-room clerk, and was subsequently promoted sergeant. The work of equipping, organising and training were hurried on, the new guns tested on the range, and at length, on August 6th, the Squadron was inspected with the Brigade by General Bailloud.

On August 8th, Capt. E. Davies (previously with the 7th Brigade in Egypt) arrived from "leave" in the United Kingdom, and was posted to the Squadron as "second in command". Orders were received on August 10th that the Brigade would move to the Palestine front on the 12th— within a month of the M.G. Squadron being formed!

CHAPTER 2

Trek to Amr, Through the Desert of Sinai

The forthcoming continuous trek (which lasted 18 days) through the desert at the hottest time of the year was no light task for a new unit to contemplate, and the two days in which to make all the preparations were none too many; yet, everything was ready by the time ordered for parade, and from that moment the 20th Machine Gun Squadron became a fighting force! There was, however, a lot of training still to be done, before it could hope to play its proper part in active operations.

The organisation of the transport for the unit was one of the greatest difficulties to be overcome. No one, unless he has actually seen it, would believe the energy required to pull even a lightly loaded wheeled vehicle through the desert sand, which, in places, is of the soft "silver" variety found at many English seaside resorts.

Each "G.S." (general service) limbered wagon is designed to carry about a ton, and is drawn by 4 mules. On this occasion, however, 4 cwts. was the maximum load, and for this 6 mules were required in every case. In spite of such a team, the going was hard enough, in very truth, and sore shoulders were not uncommon, owing to the mules being so "soft," and the new breast-collars so hard!

It was not long before the advantage a "M.G." Squadron possesses, in being able to change "pack" mules to "draught" and vice versa, was seen, this method relieving sore shoulders and sore backs by one simple operation. Although an early start was made every day, many miles had to be traversed with the sun right overhead; the afternoon was usually well advanced before the horses had been watered, lines put down, and shelters erected, blankets, rifles, bayonets and bits of string being used for this purpose.

It may here be mentioned that, at this time, the Kantara Military Railway had been completed as far as Shellal, and whilst on the march, rations and forage were drawn from "dumps" which had been placed at intervals along the line. As regards drinking water, this was brought up every day on camels. The supply of water was not too plentiful by any means, and it required a certain amount of care and self-restraint to make it last the appointed time, in fact, strict water-discipline was very necessary among all ranks. It was a tired but wiser Squadron that arrived at Amr! Many were the difficulties that had been overcome, and many the hardships that had been silently endured!

The following were the days' marches in August 1917:

12th to El Ferdan
13th to Kantara (Hill 70). Long day in great heat
14th at Kantara drawing ordnance stores
15th to Pelusium 13 miles
16th to Romani 7 miles. Heavy going
17th to Khirba 14 miles
18th to Bir el Abd 7 miles. Heavy going
19th to Tilul, watering at Salmana
20th to Bir el Masar 8 miles
21st to Maadan 15 miles. Very heavy going and particularly hot
22nd to Bardawil 8 miles. Good going
23rd to El Arish 8 miles. Heavy going
24th Rested

25th to El Burd 11 miles
26th to Sheikh Zowaid, by the shore. Very heavy
27th to Rafa
28th at Rafa obtaining stores which were sent forward by rail
29th to Amr into camp, 1 mile south of railway.

CHAPTER 3
The Squadron at Amr

Having arrived at Amr, further progress was made in the training of the unit. Each day one man was "told off" to three animals, the remainder thus being free for work on the gun. The "horse-men" did one hour on the gun, remainder of day on animals. "Gun-numbers" worked one hour at stables and the remainder of the day on the gun. The daily routine was as follows:—Reveille 04.30; Parades, 06.30 to 10.00 and 15.00 to 17.30. Horses were watered twice (from troughs at the railway), and fed four times a day.

As early as September 8th, there was a test "turn-out" of the Squadron in full marching order, with guns on packs. The new regulations regarding rations and forage included "Iron" and two days' emergency-rations (in wallets) for the man, and one day's emergency-forage (9 lbs. of grain), in a "sandbag" rolled in a ground-sheet and carried on the front arch of the saddle, for the horse, in addition to the two days' forage carried in the nosebags; furthermore one day's rations and forage were carried on the wagons. The time taken for the turn-out was actually 2 hours 10 minutes. No doubt many members who read this will smile at the recollection of the incident—and well they might! Three days later the Squadron paraded in exactly half that time, and when, on September 13th, there was a test Divisional "turn-out," all that was needed was 44 minutes—not a bad achievement for marching-order with nothing ready!

On September 13th the formation of a fourth Sub-section was approved. It was just about this time that the "Khamseen" became very troublesome. This is a strong wind that blows at this season of the year, particularly in the afternoon. The soil at Amr being a mixture of fine sand and dust, the result can be better imagined than described; it was so bad that on two days training was entirely suspended.

"Mounted" training was started on September 22nd, and in the absence, at that time, of any "set" official-drill (one actually did exist, but was known only to those who had passed through the Machine-Gun Cavalry training centre in England of whom there were not half-a-dozen in the Squadron), the O.C. (Capt. D. Marshall) thought out, and perfected, a drill that was easy to pick up, and was one which, in all respects, fulfilled requirements. Everything was proceeding most satisfactorily, the men were keen, and, towards the end of September, firing practice was started on a 25-yard range. Everybody fired the course.

In a Machine-Gun Squadron every man is mounted on a horse (some Squadrons, however, had mules for draught as did the "20th"), except the cooks, who are allowed bicycles. As the speed of bicycles in the middle of a desert proved to be quite out of proportion to the labour expended, 13 donkeys were finally issued in lieu thereof. These splendid little animals were found to be very useful, besides providing a source of amusement for a long time to come. In camp they would play about just like dogs, standing up on their hind legs and romping about with each other. The natives' usual method of riding a donkey in the East is rather comical. They sit well to the rear, in fact right over the hind-quarters, and with their feet forward, these they wave in and out between the animal's legs, and thereby make him increase his pace. A turn to either flank is accomplished by their hitting him on the neck with a stick, or putting their toe in his eye!

On October 1st-3rd "A" Sub-section went on a reconnaissance with the Brigade, which, however, was "in support" at Reshid Beck, and not called upon for active work. Meanwhile the training continued—Squadron drill, section schemes and N.C.O.'s rides. The completion of the Squadron to the full establishment of six Sub-sections (12 guns) was sanctioned on October 9th, although the supply of horses was stated to be doubtful. On that date the Squadron was inspected by the G.O.C. the Brigade, Brig.-Gen. J.T. Wigan, C.M.G., D.S.O.

CHAPTER 4

Draft from Maresfield Park, England

Lieut. Raynor arrived with 47 "O.R.'s" on Oct. 9th. These were part of a draft of 15 officers and 250 men under Capt. R.O. Hutchinson, who had left England on September 13th. Before starting on their journey the draft had been complimented upon their appearance by the C.O. of the Training Centre, and told that "they should consider themselves lucky to be going to a country where real cavalry tactics could be employed". And so it proved to be! This draft arrived at Alexandria on September 27th, and proceeded to the M.G.C. Base Depot, Helmieh, Cairo, after a very pleasant but uneventful journey, via Southampton, Havre, Marseilles and Malta. The journey through France was by a route not previously used for troops, and the French people were very friendly and enthusiastic, cheering frequently. Apparently the population here were not accustomed to the sight of British troops. At Marseilles they embarked on H.M.T. *Minetonka* (a splendid ship, but very crowded), which, being built for the North-Atlantic traffic, was rather hot for the Mediterranean. Two very efficient Japanese destroyers escorted her throughout the whole journey.

At first, it was thought that the "draft" was intended to form an entirely new unit, but they had not long been in Egypt before officers and men were posted to various existing Squadrons. The importance of this draft is indicated, to some extent, by the fact that within a short time every Machine Gun Squadron in the E.E.F. (except one), was commanded by an officer who had come out with it.

CHAPTER 5

Preparations for War

Early in October 1917, the C.O.'s of units were informed
of the approaching operations against the enemy, and given
a general idea of the plan of campaign. On the 17th of the
month, Headquarters and three Sub-sections marched, with
the Brigade, across the desert to Bir el Esani. The country,
up to this point, was patrolled by the Imperial Camel Corps
(I.C.C.), and it might be termed the limit of the country so
far in British occupation, as, at Esani, patrols of British and
Turks were frequently in the habit of watering their horses
in the wadi when the other was not about! The next day
(October 18th), a reconnaissance was made across the Wadi
Mirtaba and towards Goz-el-Naam. "B" and "C" Sub-sections were attached to the "S.R.Y." and "S.N.H." but saw
no "targets" to justify the opening of machine-gun fire. "A"
Sub-section was in reserve. The following day (the 19th),
the Brigade returned to Amr. The experience gained by the
Machine Gun Squadron during these operations proved to
be most valuable; the animals were fit, but certainly rather
fagged; the transport was found to be too heavily loaded,
and the pack-animals were also tired.

Orders were now received that when operations started

the Squadron would move out five Sub-sections strong. This would mean a severe test for "D" and "E" Sub-sections. "D" Sub-section under Lieut. Raynor, was well in hand, although only formed a few weeks previously, but the equipment for "E" (and "F") had only just been drawn!

On October 20th, Lieut. Price, M.C., Lieut. Millman and Sec.-Lieut. Kindell (all from the recent draft from Maresfield) arrived at the Camp. Lieut. Price at once took over the organization of "E"; Lieut. Millman was nominally posted to "F" and Sec.-Lieut. Kindell supernumerary, for the time being. It could hardly be said that the formation of "E" Sub-section had been "rushed"! The term is hardly suitable— "Cyclonic" would be nearer the mark! It literally had horses and equipment issued to it one day, and was fighting the next. At length, on October 25th, definite orders were received for the first phase of the projected operations against Beersheba to be undertaken, and, the next day, Sec.-Lieut. Kindell and three O.R.'s (Ptes. Carr, Ineson and Marshall), with representatives from other units of the Brigade, proceeded with the Staff Captain and Brigade Intelligence Officer, to Esani, in order to "take-over" the camping area and reconnoitre the outpost-line there.

Lieut. Macmillan and five O.R.'s (Ptes. J. Howlett, A. Jacques, S. Morris, A. Tivey and E.A. Riley), who were chosen as stout-hearted men, reported to Col. Newcombe, R.E., D.S.O., at Gamli, for special duty. Bad luck attended them, however! The whole party was captured a few days later.

The following is the official account of this adventure:

> To assist in completing the rout of the Turkish troops retiring from Beersheba, a small mobile force on camels, consisting of Lewis gunners, machine gunners, and a few Sudanese Arab scouts, under Lieut.-Col. S.F. Newcombe, R.E., D.S.O., left Asluj on October 30. It had a number of machine guns and Lewis guns, a large quan-

tity of small-arms ammunition, and carried three days' rations. Moving rapidly, it established its headquarters at Yutta, and on October 31 occupied some high ground west of, and commanding the road between Dhaheriyeh and Hebron. It was hoped that the Turks, retiring by night from Beersheba, would encounter this force, which, taking them by surprise, would, by its large fire-power put them to rout, and cause a general débâcle on the Turkish left-wing. However, as the Anzac Mounted Division had cut the road further south, the Turkish forces from Beersheba retired north to Tel esh Sheria. The force, nevertheless, succeeded in intercepting and capturing the motor transport with supplies, which was endeavouring to reach Beersheba from Jerusalem.

The Turks were surprised by the appearance of this force, and having no idea of its numbers, despatched the 12th Depot Regiment from Hebron, and the 143rd Regiment from Tel esh Sheria—six battalions in all—to dislodge it. It held out resolutely, but, after sustaining heavy casualties and having exhausted all its ammunition, was obliged to surrender on November 2 or 3.

The personnel (32 O.R.'s) and equipment of "F" Subsections, were sent to "Brigade Details" at Gamli under Lieut. Millman, no horses being then available.

CHAPTER 6

The Beersheba Campaign

On the morning of October 28th 1917, the Squadron marched from Amr, across the 16 miles of desert to Esani. It consisted of:

> Seven officers, 182 men, 10 guns, 156 riding horses, 70 draught and 31 pack animals, 13 donkeys; with transport of ("A" Echelon), water cart, 12 limbered G.S. wagons; ("B.1" Echelon) three L.G.S. wagons, carrying reserve day's forage and rations; ("B.2" Echelon) one G.S. wagon.

So far as can be ascertained now, the following were the W.O. and N.C.O.'s of the Squadron at this time:

> **Headquarters**: S.S.M. Larwood, S.Q.M.S. Harrison, Far.-Sergt. Robertson, Transport-Sergt. Conuel, Sig.-Corpl. Billam, S.S.-Corpl. Holmes, Saddler-Corpl. Mellett.
>
> **"A" Sub-section**: Sergt. Fisher, Lance-Corpl. Rouse, Lance-Corpl. Keetley.
>
> **"B" Sub-section**: Sergt. Potts, Corpl. Hazlehurst, Lance-Corpl. Hughes, Lance-Corpl. Peadon.
>
> **"C" Sub-section**: Sergt. Wright, Corpl. Gill, Nos. 1. Pte. S. Kidd, Pte. P. Lee.
>
> **"D" Sub-section**: Sergt. Fleet, Corpl. Barrett, Lance-Corpl. Green, Lance-Corpl. Marriott.

"E" Sub-section: Sergt. O'Neill, Corpl. Franklin, Lance-Corpl. Grice, Lance-Corpl. Thompson.

Upon arrival at their destination, everyone who had previously been there, on reconnaissance, was struck by the great changes that had taken place within such a short time; the locality had, in fact, become one huge camp. There were armoured cars, R.E.s, motor-tractors, besides thousands of camels—indeed, every branch of the service was represented. Incidentally, it may be mentioned that these preparations were not hidden from the Turks, whose aeroplanes came over every day and dropped bombs, without, however, doing much damage.

The camping site for the Squadron proved to be in a wide gully, leading up from the Wadi Ghuzze, between two hills. After watering in the wadi (to reach which a rather steep slope had to be negotiated), "lines" were put up and the new bivouac sheets recently issued, erected, after which, having had something to eat, the Squadron was able to enjoy a well-earned rest. In the very early hours of the following morning "C" Sub-section, under Sec.-Lieut. Kindell (who now took command in the absence of Lieut. Macmillan), proceeded with the "S.R.Y." to take up the day outpost-line some few miles north-east of Reshid Beck. It soon became evident that the Turk had intended to occupy this line, as he contested it with rifle fire; he was, however, just a little too late and had to withdraw! The position we now occupied afforded splendid observation of all the surrounding country. In fact, the ground dropped abruptly to a plain several miles wide, cut by wadis and studded with low mounds; on the right the Wadi Ghuzze with a narrow stream of water on one side, wended its way across the plain, almost to our lines.

On the other side of the plain, on the banks of the wadi, the tents of a Turkish camp could plainly be seen, and (by the aid of a pair of field glasses), the Turks themselves, going about their work. During the day various officers from an infantry division came up to the post in order to view the ground, over which, they stated, they were going to attack, in two days' time. At dusk our troops withdrew through the night-outpost line; "C" Sub-section, with the one limber that accompanied it, returned to camp, independently. On this day the Squadron watering-party was bombed by hostile aircraft, but no casualties occurred. October 30th was spent in "resting," and in the afternoon every man was directed to lie down in his "bivvy" from 13.00 to 17.00 hrs. (1 p.m. to 5 p.m.)! Upon being asked by the Orderly Officer why he was not complying with this order, one man remarked to his pal: "Well, that's the first time I've been stopped doing work in the Army"! It was, however, very necessary, as, that night at 20.30 (8.30 p.m.), the Brigade, commanded by Brig.-Gen. J.T. Wigan, C.M.G., D.S.O., started on its approach-march after watering.

CHAPTER 7

The March to Beersheba

The "going" was, most of the way, through thick sand with a lot of green scrub. Doubtless, everybody who took part in that march will ever remember the incidents and details of the operations—and the indescribable dust. Temperature very cold; "loads off"; "loads on"; at frequent intervals. So—on, through the night; generally at the walk, occasionally trotting; hearing, at one point, intermittent rifle-fire (on the left flank), and, with now and the *very lights* being put up. Later on, a white stone building was passed (apparently unoccupied) called "Ibn Said".

After several hours' marching, a road and a narrow gauge Turkish railway were crossed, both of which were understood to lead to Beersheba. At length, the position was reached on Itwail El Semin, 7 miles south of Beersheba, just before daybreak, where the transport ("A" Echelon) soon found us. "A" and "B" Sub-sections were immediately attached to the "S.R.Y." and "S.N.H." respectively, and took up positions in front of Ras-Hablein and Goz-el-Naam.

It was not long before it became evident that there was "something doing". Yes, the great event for which the Squadron had been preparing since its formation was about to take place! The 7th Mounted Brigade found itself "up against" a series of strongly-held trenches on Ras-Hablein to Ras-Ghannam. The 60th Infantry Division was on its left and the Australians on its right. The plan of attack, as given in the official publication: *A Brief Record of the Advance of the Egyptian Expeditionary Force* was as follows:

> ... for the 60th and 74th Divisions to seize the enemy works between the Khalasa Road and the Wadi Saba, while the defences north of the Wadi were masked by the Imperial Camel Corps Brigade and two battalions of the 53rd Division. The Anzac Mounted Division, Australian Mounted Division and 7th Mounted Brigade were to attack the defences of the town from the north-east, east and south-east.

The progress of the attack all along the line could be seen from the top of Itwail. The Turk, everywhere, clung tenaciously to his main positions. During the whole morning and afternoon, rifle and shell-fire were continued on both sides. "B" Sub-section covered the advance of the "S.N.H." The Essex Battery R.H.A., in action at this time, came in for a bad quarter of an hour, but fortunately escaped with slight casualties, when, at 16.00 (4 p.m.) orders were issued to attack Beersheba!

The Brigade at once formed up in a cloud of dust, and, led by its General as if on a ceremonial parade at home, started off at the trot to the attack. Soon, the dust became so dense (especially in the centre of the Brigade), that it was impossible to see two yards in front. After going a mile or two, a halt was made under cover of a hill for a few minutes, then on again. To the surprise of everyone, little opposition was now offered, and it soon became apparent that the Turk had fled, although reinforced during the day, the sight of an English Cavalry Brigade advancing, proving too much for him! Another halt, another trot, then the position was taken!

CHAPTER 8

We Take Beersheba

Until quite recently, the Turk had been content merely to patrol the country south and east of Beersheba, but our concentration at Esani had made him uneasy about his left flank, and he had hastily dug a line of trenches and manned them, hoping to put up a strong opposition to our advance. These were the trenches we had now taken; and they constituted a strong position too, the hills being particularly steep in front of them.

Having captured the position and enjoyed a short rest, the Brigade pushed on again after dark—this time in column of route, but "at the walk," as it was "pitch-black" and the ground rough and rocky. Well on in the evening, a welcome change in the going occurred, as we came out upon a road (the same one crossed in the morning); a proper road, a real road like one at home in England! It seemed strange, indeed, after the miles of desert; the horses appreciated it too! Later, the moon having risen, a long halt was made, after which the road towards Beersheba was resumed. Every mile or so, by the wayside were now passed remains of Turkish camps, dead animals, overturned wagons, abandoned ammunition, etc., etc. The enemy had evidently left in "some" haste. But there were still isolated parties of the enemy in the hills, from which direction shots could be heard from time to time.

After a long and gruelling journey, during which everyone was dead tired and the horses badly in need of water, the outskirts of the "town" of Beersheba were at last reached. Here the Squadron halted, whilst the units in front "watered". It then became known to us that Beersheba had already been occupied by the Australians, who, no doubt, had come in from the flank. As regards the "water," this was contained in a long stone trough, and, although it was thick with mud, it was all that could be had. Yet, of this filth the animals drank deeply, not having tasted a drop of liquid for 24 hours!

After "watering," a camping-area for the night was allotted to the Squadron near by. The animals having been off-saddled and fed, everyone was glad to be able to lie down in his clothes and snatch some sleep during the few remaining hours, until it was time to "stand to" in the morning. Before daybreak the Squadron saddled-up and moved off into the plain outside the town. Here it halted in "Line of Sub-section Column" and dismounted. No sooner had the sun risen, however, when machine-gun fire broke out from all directions. At once the order was given to extend for rifle fire. Everyone expected to see the dust thrown up all round by the thousands of bullets which were being fired, and prepared for a great mêlée, but—nothing happened! A perfect tornado of fire and nothing whatever could be seen! After a few minutes, to the surprise of all, everything was quiet again! The explanation was obtained afterwards: all that had happened was that a Boche plane had appeared over our outpost line. He must, certainly, have had a hot reception!

Then "lines" were put down, animals off-saddled again and a much needed wash-up and shave indulged in—after watering and stables. To feel clean once more and to be able to have a sleep in the heat of the day, which at this time was intense (in spite of the cold nights), was a treat enjoyed by all.

Beersheba was very disappointing. Instead of being a town, as Europeans understand that term, a place where one can buy such things as cigarettes and something to eat, nothing at all was obtainable, and the only buildings in it, that were not mud huts, were empty.

During our stay at Beersheba, enemy planes, often flying quite low, paid us several visits, for whose benefit one Sub-section always had its guns mounted for anti-aircraft work. On one of these raids two men and several animals, in an Australian Field Ambulance a couple of hundred yards from the Squadron Camp, were killed. One man had a "narrow shave". He was standing beside his horse when the plane appeared, and, for safety, he jumped into a trench that happened to be at hand still holding the reins. The animal was killed, but he himself escaped without a scratch!

CHAPTER 9

The Coastal Sector

To the 21st Infantry Corps in front of Gaza, had been given the task of attracting enemy reserves to that neighbourhood, thus to lighten the task of the troops on the right of the line, in the capture of Beersheba. On October 27th, a bombardment of the elaborate Gaza defences had been commenced, assisted by the Navy, and on the night of November 1st-2nd, "Umbrella Hill" was captured, followed in the early morning by the whole of the front-line system of trenches.

After a day's rest, the 7th Mounted Brigade started off again (on November 2nd) at 08.30. "C" Sub-section reported to the "S.N.H."; "D" Sub-section to the "S.R.Y." The Transport ("B.1" Echelon) just arrived as the Squadron was timed to move off, and rations had to be issued out on parade. [It may here be mentioned that the transport had had a "rough time," and without having accurate knowledge of what was happening to the Brigade, owing to the many difficulties of communication en route, did splendidly in arriving even when it did.]

The railway being crossed, the Brigade "carried on," along a sort of old track north of Beersheba for about 10 miles, where a halt was called. A short description of the country hereabouts would not, perhaps, be out of place. Doubtless other people will read this record besides the members of the Squadron who have seen the "beauties" of that remote part of the world; a brief reference to the characteristics of the locality may, therefore, be appreciated by those who would like to spend a short holiday there!

Now, the ground itself, baked hard by the tropical sun and total absence of water, is covered with stones, it has practically no vegetation whatever, any scrub, at all resembling a tree, being something to remark upon. Parts of the country, however, are cultivated by the natives during the winter and spring, but at the time of our campaign everything was quite bare. Then, there are no roads; the tracks made by the natives are inches deep in dust, which, when used by troops, rises in dense clouds, choking one's nose and eyes, besides "caking" on the face, so that in a very short time every man more resembles a performer in a minstrel troupe rather than a soldier in His Majesty's Army. Everywhere hills are to be seen, upon which there are outcrops of rock. Upon these hills, also, a small bushy plant manages to grow (a kind of thyme), which has a very pungent smell.

In front of the halting place, mentioned above, was a plain about a mile wide; on each side of this was a range of hills. The "S.R.Y." and "D" Sub-section made towards Khuweilfeh on their left front, and the "S.N.H." and "C" Sub-section set off half-right towards the hills. The "S.N.H." met but slight opposition from the enemy, which they easily overcame. Pushing forward and taking, on the way, two field-guns and two ambulances abandoned by the Turks, they, at length, gained the highest point (Ras en Nukb); from here could be seen the Turkish position on the other side of the plain, being attacked by the "S.R.Y."

It was clear that no further advance could be made until the Turks on the left were dislodged. This seemed to be a difficult proposition, as enemy reinforcements could be seen coming up in great numbers. Towards evening an attempt was made to attack them on the other side, but the ground being found to be very rocky, and after being shelled considerably and night setting in, orders were received to withdraw. Then the "S.N.H." came right back to the point where they had left the Brigade, and "C" Sub-section remained with them for that night. After several attempts had been made to bring in the captured guns, it was decided it was impossible to retain them, so they were turned over a precipice.

The next morning (November 3rd) before daylight, the "S.N.H." and "C" Sub-section set out again, and occupied the same position which they had evacuated the previous night, being relieved about 10.00 by the Australians. They had, however, to stand-by for a time, as the Turks showed signs of attacking. On the way back to the Brigade they passed British infantry on the way up to the attack, moving under artillery fire, which on both sides was very lively just then.

In the meantime "D" Sub-section had been having an adventure; the following incident being related by one who was present:

> Shortly after leaving the Brigade, we came into action on a ridge and gave overhead fire, while the S.R.Y. attacked the enemy position which was on another ridge about 1,800 yards off. After a short time, in order to get closer to the enemy, we advanced to an intervening ridge about 900 yards, bringing us this distance from the enemy. During this advance, which was carried out at the gallop, we were subjected to very heavy machine-gun fire, through which we were lucky to come with the loss of only one pack mule. The second position was a good one, and we were able to bring very effective fire on to the enemy who were in a similar position to ourselves, only rather higher up. Observation was very bad owing to the hard ground.

After being in action for a considerable time and having fired a large quantity of ammunition, we suddenly became aware that we were entirely "on our own," not one S.R.Y. or a man of any other unit to be seen. Mr. Raynor went back to try to re-establish communication, and just as it was rapidly getting dark he sent up an orderly to tell us to come out of action, and to lead us down into a gulley below the position we held, where he was. When we arrived at what the guide thought was the spot, however, it was quite dark, indeed "pitch black". He was nowhere to be found, and after sending out scouts in all directions, and still being unable to find him in the darkness, we took the opportunity to feed the horses. After a short rest and being under the impression that the Brigade had advanced (from information previously obtained) we advanced too! After passing our former position, and descending the steep slope beyond, we at last sighted a light, and sent out a man (Pte. Chantry) to reconnoitre. Our surprise can be imagined, when he got to within a hundred yards of it he was fired at. It was a party of Turks! They immediately 'stood to' and let us have it 'hot'. We at once galloped to cover on the left flank, but unfortunately before we reached it Francis was hit, and we never saw the poor chap again! The pack animal he was leading, however, came along with the rest of the horses.

Just after this incident a gun 'pack' (the Bint), got loose (she was always difficult to lead), and galloped off. But she came in by herself the next morning, followed shortly afterwards by the horse poor Francis had been riding when he met his end. After we reached cover, we found the 'S.R.Y.' Headquarters close by, so we reported there, when we were told that orders had been issued for us to re-join the Squadron. The 'O.C.' and Mr. Raynor were there also, who told us to remain for the night, off-saddling half at a time. The following morning we again came into action near our original position of the previous day, but did not fire. During the morning we were relieved by some machine guns from the Camel Corps, and then rejoined the Brigade.

"B" Sub-section was early attached to the Australians and advanced, on the right of the "S.R.Y.," on the edge of the plain. They had tough fighting and fired a considerable quantity of ammunition. It is regretted that information is not available, to allow of a detailed description of the adventures of this Sub-section at Khuweilfeh, being given. It is certain, however, that the Sub-section rendered the Australians valuable assistance, which was greatly appreciated.

The Brigade, having been relieved by the 53rd Division, now commenced the long march back to Beersheba, a distance of at least 10 miles, through the country we have just described. This journey, and that which followed, were the most tiring of these operations. It must be remembered that the horses had not been watered nor the men's water-bottles filled, since the previous morning. When the intense heat of the day is considered, not to mention the dust, the hardships suffered can, perhaps, be imagined! The G.O.C. (Brig.-Gen. J.T. Wigan, C.M.G., D.S.O.) went along the whole column and handed his brandy-flask to those who seemed the most exhausted. Upon arriving at Beersheba, the town was found to be swarming with more troops, and it was with the greatest difficulty that any water was obtained at all. Everyone had gone without just as long as we had done—at least, so they said!

The next day (November 4th), was spent in watering and cleaning up. Towards evening, "Saddle-up" was ordered; the Brigade moved at 16.00 and marched to Karm, a distance of 15 miles—a journey which seemed interminable. The air was so thick with dust that it was necessary to keep right on to the tail of the horse in front, or you would have been lost in a second. "'Ware hole on the right!" "Mind the wire!" and such like orders were passed down the column from time to time. You had just to do what you were told, as it was quite impossible to see even a yard ahead!

Arrived at Karm, at about 22.00, the Brigade watered

their horses from the troughs beside the railway line, which were supplied with water brought up in trucks by train from the pipe line at Shellal or El Arish! After a short sleep, the Brigade moved on a few miles to Goz el Geleib, and took over a camping area from the 8th Mounted Brigade.

Our Squadron took over the identical ground just occupied by the 21st Squadron, and the small party we sent on in advance learnt of the action they had been in, when strongly attacked, and the praise they had earned from the Commander-in-Chief. During this action, one of their officers (Lieut. Stuart) who was known to some of the members of the "20th," was captured. He was at first reported killed.

The Brigade stayed here for the day in reserve. Glad enough everyone was of this little rest, which at any time is indeed "very little" for a cavalry unit, even when halted. That afternoon an officer of the Squadron was ordered to proceed to a point overlooking the Wadi Imleh and establish signalling communication with the Australian Headquarters, and to keep watch for any enemy movement across it. The line, in this part, was held by small posts, in some places over a mile apart. It would seem to be an easy matter for the Turk to creep up during the night and at daybreak pour through the gaps. It was, indeed, at this point that the 21st Squadron had been so hard pressed.

Nothing unusual happened on this occasion, however, and the next morning (November 6th), the Brigade moved at 08.30 to a point north-east of Karm, near Abu Irgeig, just behind the line. Two sub-sections were at once sent to a line of observation overlooking Wadi Imleh. Persistent rumours of an enemy attack from this quarter which, as has been seen, was very lightly held, kept everyone on the alert.

"C" Sub-section watered at Karm during the day and before night the positions were carried by the infantry and the Brigade camped near by. But it was on the move again the next morning (November 7th) long before daylight (at 04.30). No person in the Squadron knew what was the destination, and when, at length, day broke, there were many speculations even as to the locality they were then actually in.

Eventually a railway was crossed, and the country appeared just like that north of Beersheba. It transpired, in fact, that they were only a few miles from that town, but on a different road from that leading to Khuweilfeh. After having covered about 8 miles since the morning, the Brigade approached Tel-el-Sheria, where it came in sight of the railway station, and under enemy shell-fire, which was pretty hot at times. At the station itself the shelling was hotter still, as 5.9's were falling thick just there. At night, however, all shelling ceased and the troops were able to water their horses at 23.00 in the wadi, close to the station.

Meanwhile at Gaza, on the coast, the intense bombardment of the Turkish lines that had been going on, was more than the enemy could stand, and he began to withdraw his troops. To such an extent had the withdrawal been carried out, that a British attack on the night of November 6th-7th met with but slight opposition, and Outpost Hill, Middlesex Hill and Ali-Munter were captured without much trouble. The Imperial Service Cavalry Brigade passed right through the ruins of Gaza.

CHAPTER 10

The Brigade Advances

The following day (November 8th), at 05.00, a further advance was made by our Brigade along the railway about 9 miles, and the enemy was sighted in the neighbourhood of Tel Hudeiwe, whom the "S.N.H." and "C" Sub-section were sent to dislodge. This task they accomplished at once, but a sudden counter-attack forced back our advanced points with a rush, who sustained some casualties. The position then held was a good one, and there were little doubts about our being able to hold it, even if outnumbered. The ground was so steep in the rear, that led-horses could be brought up to within 20 yards, or less, of the guns. In front, too, the ground sloped away sharply, and on the other side of the valley was a ridge, similar to our own, to which the Turks had withdrawn, and where they could be seen in large numbers. They kept up a very heavy rifle and machine-gun fire, which, however, we heartily returned. Their artillery, evidently, was being employed elsewhere, as will be shown shortly. During the afternoon the Turks were seen to be reinforced, and showed every sign of attempting an attack. "B" Sub-section came up and was in action alongside "C"; "E" Sub-section also was attached, but was held in reserve for eventualities. It was soon seen, however, that the Turk had come to the conclusion that "discretion was the better part of valour," for nothing further happened.

Meanwhile "D" Sub-section had been having a rough time. They had taken up a position close to Brigade Headquarters with the Essex Battery, to protect it from a flank attack. The Essex and Turkish artillery had a lively duel, during which shells fell thick, around this quarter. Lance-Corpl. Marriott was, unfortunately, killed, while Lieut. Raynor, Ptes. Taylor and Crane, and, later, Lance-Corpl. Green, were wounded, in this action. It may be mentioned here, that Lieut. Raynor was hit in the arm, and after undergoing several operations in Nasrieh Hospital, Cairo, he was sent home and finally retired from the Army. The manner in which he had organised "D" Sub-section, and in a few weeks made it a fighting unit of exceptional quality, had earned him great praise. Sergt. Fleet, who assumed command after Lieut. Raynor was hit, did splendid work and was afterwards awarded the Military Medal.

All was quiet during the night, and at daybreak the patrols sent out, reported "all clear"; the Turks had "Imshied" (i.e., cleared out). After watering, under a certain amount of shell fire, the Sub-sections that had been in the line rejoined the Squadron; the remainder had watered late the previous night, and were not allowed the time to water again. Then commenced an exciting race across country towards the coast, in an endeavour to cut off the Turkish garrison at Gaza, which was stated at this time to be in full retreat. The Brigade advanced 16 miles that day—"Point 375," Simsin-Bureir, Huliekht, Julis—right through the ancient land of the Philistines.

A different kind of country was being met with now, much of it being, evidently, cultivated during certain times of the year. Many villages were also passed, some of which looked quite pretty from a distance, clustering among their cactus hedges and a few trees. But anything green would have looked pleasant at that moment to the men who, for so long, had seen nothing but the arid desert. It was a case, however, of "distance lending enchantment to the view", as a close inspection proved disappointing. The filth in which these people live must be seen to be realised. Language fails in this case! Their houses are simply mud huts consisting, generally, of only one room, in which the whole family live! During the day strong healthy men sit about outside, while the women do all the work, even to the toilsome labour of tilling the ground! A search for water in such places is not a very hopeful matter; at the most there might be two wells, from which water could be got up, a bucketful at a time—a hopeless look out, when there are thousands of thirsty men and horses! Nothing was seen of the enemy that day, and when the sea came in view (what a splendid sight!), it was evident the Gaza forces had escaped.

What an enormous amount of ammunition and stores they had left behind! It has been stated, unofficially, it would have been enough to last them 12 months! Evidently, the enemy did not expect to leave in such a hurry.

That night the Brigade bivouacked at Julis, and the next morning (November 10th), in attempting to water "B" Sub-section was shelled out of Es Suafir el Gharbiye. The Squadron then returned to Julis, and was ordered to off-saddle and look for water at one of the villages near the coast. Eventually they found a moderate supply at Hamame, 3-1/2 miles away, together with—quite unexpectedly—oranges. To say that these were appreciated is hardly adequate, it can well be imagined that they were a luxury just then!

Having returned to camp, Capt. Davies and Lieut. Price

excited the envy of the other officers. They had been to El-Mejdel, a few miles south of Hamame, which turned out to be quite civilised compared with the surrounding villages, and they had bought some tobacco and, actually, had had a cup of coffee!

Chapter 11
Rest at Hamame

An hour or two afterwards we had great news! The Brigade was to go to Hamame for a rest and clean up, and perhaps a swim in the sea! After our experiences it would certainly be difficult to think of anything that could be more appreciated, unless it were a square meal; but then, there were oranges to be had, to make up for shortcomings in that respect.

Only 11 days since leaving Esani, yet how much had been crowded into that short period! As much work had been done every day as was usually done in a week. It was not the fatigue of the trekking and fighting that "told" so much, but the lack of adequate rest; generally "turning-in" very late at night, and often having to sleep in boots ready to move before daylight the following morning, with nothing but "bully beef," biscuits, and (a very little) jam to eat. Sometimes tea was available, but frequently without sugar or milk. As regards "bully beef," this may be very sustaining, but it is a fact difficult to believe when having nothing else to eat for weeks on end. The look of it was enough to make one sick! Of course, in the circumstances, no other rations were possible, and the Supply Department certainly did wonders to keep units supplied with any kind of food, when they did not know, from one hour to another, where they would be located next, without taking into consideration the distances that had to be covered over roads hardly worthy to be called tracks.

Two days were spent at Hamame, and how glorious they were! The Squadron rode down "bare-back" to the beach each day (two miles away) and bathed, the horses going into the sea as well. They were watered from wells just dug by the Field Troop (R.E.). It is a curious fact that all along this coast one has only to dig down in the sand a few feet, and there an inexhaustible supply of fresh water is to be found. It only remains to put up canvas troughs and hand pumps, and any number of horses can be watered, as easily as if they were in the best watered country in the world. It is unfortunate that this is not possible away from the coast.

CHAPTER 12

In the Line

At 04.30 on the morning of November 13th, the Brigade moved from its comfortable quarters at Hamame, nearly due east to Beit Affe, and then beyond Summeil, where a line was taken over which had been previously held by another Brigade. On the way the Turks shelled us heavily. It is surprising how difficult it is to hit a Brigade on the move, in "Line of Troop Column"; shells often fell right in the centre of a Regiment, yet not actually hitting a troop or doing any damage whatever! At night we withdrew from the line, marched on to Tel-et-Turmus, northwest, and slept there in a deep wadi. The next day at 05.30 we were "on the move" again and pushed on to El Tine crossing the railway. It was evident, from the amount of kit, dead animals, etc., on the road, that "Johnny Turk" had not been dawdling by the way!

From El Tine we went to Kezaze and thence to Junction Station where our eyes were gladdened by the sight of a *brick building*. On reaching the crest of the ridge the railway leading to Jerusalem suddenly came into view, and, parallel with it, was seen the main road to that town. Visible for several miles until lost to sight in the distant hills, it was crowded with retreating Turks who had been thoroughly surprised at our sudden appearance. The station appeared to be in flames, but the Turk was still "showing fight," and in a short time "C" Sub-section attached to the "S.R.Y." was in action on the ridge south of the railway against the enemy, who had a position on a hill the other side of it. In about a quarter of an hour, however, the Turk was seen retiring, and the Sub-section came out of action and advanced across the railway line to "let him have it" again, in his new position in front of the village of Khulde. Evening was drawing near, when orders were received to withdraw to the original position for the night, and close by there, the Squadron settled down. Before that, however, they had gone to the station to water, but the supply quickly gave out and they had to return. Towards midnight, a fresh source having been tapped, they turned out to water again, none having been had the day before: they had been 57 hours without water!

The next day no serious advance was made, but the day following, after being shelled before starting, the Brigade crossed the railway and went through Khulde, which had been evacuated. They were heavily shelled and unable to proceed, as they found the enemy firmly entrenched in the hills. "D" Sub-section got some targets at Latron. They returned to their old camp; water by this time had been developed and was no difficulty. The infantry too had arrived.

Nothing was done the next day, and everyone was glad of the rest. Sec.-Lieut. Kindell having contracted dysentery, was sent to hospital. It was now November 17th, and the Squadron had become seriously reduced in strength. More men had been lost than horses, and men leading three animals each accompanied the transport. Two officers and 50 men had been killed, wounded, or evacuated sick (more than a quarter of the whole Squadron), whereas only 15 animals had been lost. This left 35 riding horses surplus, men to lead which had to be found. It should be remembered that losses in a machine gun unit are much more serious than in a regiment. The teams for the guns have to be maintained, and when these are reduced in strength an enormous amount of extra work falls on those who remain.

At 05.30 on November 18th the Brigade went to Khurbet Deiran, 6 miles north-west, arriving the same morning.

The first sight of really civilised country was obtained at this period. On the way, the cultivated areas round Ramleh were visible as far as the eye could reach. This was indeed a very pleasant change from the barren and uncultivated tracts—the interminable stretches of rocky and boulder-strewn ground, intersected by apparently unbounded areas of flat, dust-covered wastes:

Dust in heaps and dust in piles,
Dust in shifting ridges;
Dust and dust for miles and miles,
And what 'aint dust is midges.

So quoth the cynic; and the peculiar part about it is that, wherever are large stretches of dusty ground, so also there is the wind! and nothing need be said of the result of a combat between these two forces.

All thoughts of the country left behind, however, were immediately banished from the mind at the sight of that which lay before us, and anticipation ran high in the belief that these were the wonderful orange-groves which, one had heard, were supposed to be situated in this part of Palestine. Expectations were realised, and on nearing Deiran, orchard upon orchard were passed with trees bending under the weight of hundreds of large and delicious Jaffa oranges! Everyone purchased as many as it was possible to carry, and those who had no available cash, managed to satisfy their wants by means of barter—

incidentally, be it whispered, many an odd tin of "bully" found its way into the local inhabitants' larders.

Practically the whole of this part of Palestine, reaching from Deiran to several miles north of Jaffa, is split up into a number of Jewish Colonies, settlers under the Zionist movement, and they form the nucleus of the renascent Jewish nation. Deiran was found to be a well-laid-out village composed of substantially-built houses of white stone, with red-tiled roofs, "up-to-date" furniture, and with nice white lace curtains at the windows. One could almost delude himself into the belief that he was home again. And the delusion almost became a reality as one caught sight of pretty young girls dressed in quite smart European frocks, standing in the doorways with welcoming smiles, and motherly old ladies beaming with pleasure, who handed large bunches of luscious grapes to the men as they rode by. It must be remembered that it was only two days since that the Turks had been somewhat hurriedly ejected from this place.

The great pleasure that these hard-working people experienced could be quite understood when some of the barbarous acts of the Turks are brought to mind, they being too well known to be dwelt upon here. Afterwards it was learned from the inhabitants, that many and great were the impositions placed upon them; the Turk simply took what he wanted, and should he happen to take a dislike to anyone, the latter was in danger of having all his property confiscated, without any explanation whatever being given.

The day after the Brigade arrived at Deiran they moved via Naane and Annabe to between Harmash and Nalin, 14 miles north-east. Here they stayed three days, watering twice daily, at Hadithe, about 3 miles east-north-east of Ludd. About this time the weather broke and heavy rain set in. This downpour, accompanied as it was by a considerable fall in the temperature, was a severe trial for troops attired in summer clothing who, until a few hours previously, had been suffering from excessive heat!

At 09.00 on November 23rd they went through Ludd about 16 miles south-east to Zernuka. The 24th was spent there, and on the 25th they moved in the afternoon to Rishon-le-Zion (Ayun Kara), 6 miles due north, in reserve to the Anzacs, as the enemy was becoming active in this quarter. They stayed here the following day, and men were allowed to go into the town. Rishon-le-Zion is a pretty little place, and another example of the Zionist movement. Here are large wine distilleries, and very good wine they make too! Before the War large quantities were regularly sent to England.

The next morning (November 27th), the Brigade returned to Zernuka (close to Akir). They arrived about midday and watered. Late in the afternoon Lieut. Oakley arrived, bringing 40 remounts and reinforcements for the Brigade (none for this Squadron unfortunately); he had ridden the 70 miles from Belah in 30 hours, and had, in fact, only left Cairo at 18.15 on the 24th.

CHAPTER 13

The Beit Ur Et Tahta Operations

The British line had been advanced and now extended from the River Auja north of Jaffa on the coast, south-east to a few miles north-east of Jerusalem and thence due south. The Turk at this time, although greatly demoralised, was making some desperate counter-attacks.

At 17.00 on November 27th, orders were received for a move that night at 21.00. The Brigade was required, in a great hurry, to fill a gap in the line that the Turks had discovered, and of which they appeared to intend to take advantage.

Of the Machine-Gun Squadron, only Headquarters and three sub-sections ("A" "D" and "E") were to go, but were made up to working strength by men from "B" and "C" Sub-sections. The Officer Commanding, Capt. Marshall, was there, and the "second in command," Capt. Davies. Lieut. Price, M.C., still commanded "E," but Lieut. Cazalet being sick, Lieut. Hibbert took his place in command of "A". "D" Sub-section was under Sergt. Fleet, who had just been notified that he had been awarded the Military Medal for his splendid work at Hudeiwe and elsewhere.

The forced march to Tahta (a distance of 22 miles), all through the night, after the previous operations, was "killing". The horses, however, stood the fast going over rocky ground remarkably well, and a part of the distance was even covered at the canter! A faint glimmer of dawn was just visible over the tops of the surrounding hills when the Brigade, on the morning of the 28th November, arrived, tired, dusty and dishevelled, in the vicinity of Beit ur et Tahta, a desolate native village, about 12 miles north-west of Jerusalem and situated at the end of a wadi along the centre of which ran the road leading from Jimzu.

Immediately upon arrival the horses were off-saddled and fed, the "dixies" were unearthed from off the pack-saddles and everything pointed to an early mug of tea and a much-needed rest. Unfortunately, the fates decreed otherwise, for just as the water was "on the boil" a terrific fusillade of rifle-fire broke out, seemingly from all sides. Previously to this, there had been intermittent shelling just to the north of the village, and on the commencement of the rifle-fire this increased in intensity until things began to look extremely awkward. A quick glance up at the hills surrounding the wadi gave no indication as to the source from which the firing emanated, until, a few minutes later, when several men were seen "doubling back" down the slope of the hill on the western side of the wadi. These men were afterwards found to be those holding the outposts in that particular point of the line. They came with the ominous news that the outposts were driven in and the Turks were upon us! Almost at once this was seen to be the case, as the enemy reached the top of the ridge and his fire began to take its toll of men and animals.

To gain a proper appreciation of the serious predicament in which the Brigade was placed at this moment, it will be necessary to understand the nature of the ground thereabouts. On both sides of the wadi were high banks, or hills, 60 to 80 feet high, the surface of these being strewn with large rocks and boulders. The wadi itself was about 20 yards wide with the road winding its tortuous way down the centre between rocks and boulders worn smooth by the passage of water which, ages ago, had run its course from the hills. Packed in this wadi was the Brigade, absolutely at the mercy of the withering fire of the enemy, almost from overhead.

Immediately everything became an orderly bustle and excitement. Squadrons of the two Yeomanry regiments were dispatched to take up defensive positions. The Officer Commanding ordered "E" Sub-section to come into action on the side of the hill, about 400 yards away to the left, against a Mosque which was strongly held, and whence most of the fire appeared to be coming. They "man-handled" their guns and took up good positions, the rocks affording them a certain amount of cover. The gun-teams at that time consisted of four men each, who were naturally rather exhausted after the "trek" and rush-into-action, carrying the guns.

These teams were composed as follows:

Lance-Corpl. Grice
Lance-Corpl. Thompson
Pte. Willmore
Pte. Duncan
Pte. Crossman
Pte. Joiner
Pte. Goldie
Pte. Roberts

They opened fire upon the Mosque at a range of 700 yards with good effect, silencing two enemy machine-guns.

After being in action about half-an-hour the "S.R.Y." sent to Lieut. Price to deal with a party of Turks who were bringing fire to bear on their rear. The Turks were found to be in a trench with a machine-gun. Fire was opened on them, and all were killed except one man who escaped, mounted. Attention was then directed to the Mosque, where the Turks were still causing some trouble. "Covering-fire" was given to the "S.R.Y." who attacked, but without entire success and had to withdraw. In the end the Turk was ejected, however, and he was not able again to occupy it.

During the day's fighting Pte. Crossman had been wounded.

At night both guns were placed about 50 yards apart, facing up the hill. Working hard during the night, the enemy built a breastwork on the top of the hill, and the flash of their machine-gun fire could be seen directed from that position across the front of the Mosque, apparently to prevent it being occupied. About midnight Lieut. Price was walking along the line having a look-out and had just passed his right-hand gun when he was unfortunately hit by a bullet in the groin. Lance-Corpl. Grice at once had him bandaged up and carried down to the dressing station by Ptes. Baker and Roberts. To the sorrow of all his comrades, however, he died in the Field Ambulance. He was taken to Ramleh, where he was buried.

Just after Lieut. Price was hit, Sergt. Hawkins, who had only arrived a few days previously, but rendered splendid service on this his first day's fighting, was wounded (he was afterwards awarded the Military Medal) and Corpl. Franklin then came up to take charge. He reported the casualties to Squadron Headquarters when S.S.M. Larwood came up and "took over," sending him to resume charge of the led horses.

In the morning, before daylight, the guns were moved further up the hill in line with the infantry (Scottish Rifles), who had arrived the previous evening and advanced after dark. It was during this morning's operations that Pte. Cowley was unfortunately wounded. The Turkish defenders of the breastwork, after being submitted to heavy fire, came in under a German N.C.O. and surrendered, upon which the infantry went up and occupied their late position. The infantry soon had to fall back again, however, owing to heavy shell fire, when the Turks re-occupied it. During the day there was a certain amount of bombing and sniping on both sides, during which Pte. Joiner was killed. He had been trying to account for the sniper himself, and upon being ordered to go down the hill to see about the rations for his sub-section he was hit as soon as he moved.

After dark our infantry once more attacked the position, but were again unsuccessful. At about 01.00 infantry machine-gunners came up to relieve, being shown the way by Corpl. Franklin. The guns had to be carried down to the led horses, as firing was still pretty hot; the ground, besides, was so rough that it was impossible even to lead the pack animals over it. Just before coming out of action S.S.M. Larwood and Pte. Goldie were both unfortunately wounded, the latter so seriously that he passed away six days later and was buried at Junction Station.

CHAPTER 14

"A" Sub-Section in Action

In the meantime the other Sub-sections had been "doing things" too. For example, as soon as the enemy opened fire, "A" Sub-section was detailed to join the "S.N.H." and moved over to the western side of the wadi, under cover of the hill, where this regiment was situated; orders were received to mount the guns on the top of this hill. After a difficult passage, under a heavy fire, to the position indicated, the guns were brought into action and opened fire immediately.

It was not even necessary to adjust sights, as the enemy were within "point-blank" range. Enfilading the enemy these guns were raking his flank with fire, whilst he was preparing to make a final rush down into the wadi. Had not this move been circumvented in the "nick of time," it is impossible to estimate the disastrous consequences which would have ensued. Almost at once, the deadly fire of the two machine-guns began to tell their tale, and odd Turks here and there suddenly remembered "a very urgent appointment". Within an hour the top of this hill was cleared, and the enemy were seen to be concentrating on the further ridge. From this vantage-point he kept up a brisk fire, both with machine-guns and rifles, and it was an extremely risky undertaking to show one's head above the particular rock behind which one was taking cover. Their fire, however, was returned with interest, and it helped to make "Johnny" arrive at the decision that it would be a very unwise thing to attack again that day, although he did once make a half-hearted attempt to regain his former position, which was promptly frustrated.

This state of things continued throughout the day, but the exposed position of these two guns began to make itself very evident, as the enemy's field guns, firing from the right flank, began to get the "hang of things" there. It was, indeed, only by a miracle that both gun-teams were not entirely wiped out! Night fell with the position of affairs pretty much the same, but, later on, a welcome respite was afforded by the cessation of the shell-fire, although machine-gun and rifle fire still continued, and if anything, with greater intensity.

At about midnight, a tremendous "strafe" commenced a little to the left, bombs and flares were freely used, and although no attempt was made to force the position, everything was in readiness, should the Turk have decided to do so. Our left-hand gun had been moved forward to command the approach to the ridge from which the Turks were driven earlier in the day. At daybreak enemy shells again commenced to fall, and it soon became quite apparent that no rest would be obtained that day. The enemy's artillery left little to be desired from his point of view, as regards accuracy of range, although considering the amount of shells expended our casualties were comparatively slight.

At about 2 o'clock in the afternoon, figures were observed to be moving on the top of a hill about 500 yards away on our left; they seemed to be making towards a mosque, situated at the end of the ridge. Our two machine guns were immediately turned upon them, when the whole of the hill-side suddenly became alive with Turks, who, scared out of their cover, fled to the further side of the ridge. A trench-mortar battery, which had come up during the previous night, and had taken up a position about a quarter of a mile in the rear, opened fire at once; it is feared that "Johnny" then had a very rough and uncomfortable 10 minutes. Chase was given by some troops in the vicinity, with the result that practically the whole of these enemy forces were either killed or taken prisoner. This little contretemps stirred up the wrath of "our friend the enemy" somewhat, and he strafed us continually until nightfall. At 10 o'clock, word was received that the Brigade was to be relieved, the situation now being considered well in hand; accordingly, about an hour later, a Lewis gun detachment of the Scottish Rifles took over our position, and the Sub-section then withdrew.

Meanwhile, "D" Sub-section had been strenuously engaged, and held back the enemy on their part of the line. Full advantage was taken of every target that presented itself, and heavy losses were inflicted upon the Turk.

When we first arrived at Tahta, as soon as fire was opened on us, the led-horses were saddled as quickly as possible and sent back under Sub-section Corporals to cover. They had moved off only 20 yards, when Lance-Corpl. Carr was killed. He was buried by Corpl. Rose and Pte. Wick that day, close to where the Brigade-Major was buried, a cross being, temporarily, put up to mark his grave.

The disposal of the led-horses presented a serious difficulty from the outset; their numbers were being fast reduced by casualties, and something had to be done to save them. It was impossible, obviously, to withdraw them the same way as they had been brought, the Turk having got astride of the road about half a mile below. Ultimately it was decided "to make a dash for it," and to take the horses right over the hill on the eastern side of the wadi, although while this was being done, they would be exposed even more than ever to the enemy's fire. This dangerous undertaking was, however, eventually successfully accomplished. The wadi was now, more or less, clear of men and animals, although the place was littered with killed and wounded. Here and there were to be seen animals with limbs broken, struggling to follow in the wake of their companions.

In their new position the led-horses, although rather more comfortable, were not, by any means, safe. All the "packs" and officers' horses were kept here, but the remainder, including all the horses of the regiments, were taken right back to Zernuka, or rather Akir, to which place the remainder of the Squadron left behind had moved.

At daybreak the next morning, when the enemy's artillery opened fire, the "packs" received a very severe shaking, and during the morning several of the mules were hit by shell splinters. Pte. Heathcote was killed by a shell at 10.30 whilst attending one of the wounded mules here; Pte. Rush was hit in the shoulder, an hour afterwards, and was taken to the Field Ambulance.

Upon the second (and last) night at Tahta, a very pathetic, but stirring, burial-ceremony was held at about 21.00, which those privileged to attend will remember to the end of their days. The ground selected for the burials was a little gully running off the main wadi. Dead animals, horses, mules and camels lay all around; upturned wagons and limbers were to be seen everywhere. During the deep roar and vivid flashes of our guns, just to the rear, and the sharp crack of bullets striking the rocks just above, the solemn and earnest words of our Chaplain could be heard. Above all, the full moon, bathing the gully in a bright light, combined to make a fitting background for the laying-to-rest of those who had been called upon to make the "supreme sacrifice".

On leaving Tahta the Squadron marched on foot to the

vicinity of El Burj (guns on packs), arriving before day-light (November 30th). Here they stayed for the day, in reserve, cleaning guns, etc. At 18.00, that night, they moved nearer El Burj in support of the Australians, arriving about 21.00. Nothing happened; but the Squadron stayed all night and the next day. That night they moved into El Burj; next morning (December 2nd) they returned, and found their horses awaiting them. Headquarters, "A," "D" and "E" Sub-sections now re-joined "B" and "C" Sub-sections and transport. It was not likely that the Squadron would be re-quired again in the Tahta district, except in an emergency, as the country was quite unsuitable for cavalry tactics; as it turned out, they were not destined to do any more fighting for a long time to come.

But the British advance had by no means been stopped, in spite of the check in the hills. The absence of roads and shortage of water here, made operations exceedingly diffi-cult, and it was decided to attack the Turkish positions cov-ering Jerusalem, from the south-west and west, instead of from the north-west. The troops were moved into position, and the main attack was launched at dawn on December 8th. This attack was immediately successful and resulted in the surrender of Jerusalem by the Turks to the 60th Divi-sion on the morning of Sunday, December 9th. Thus, after four centuries of conquest, the Turk was ridding the land of his presence in the bitterness of defeat. On this same day, 2082 years before, another race of conquerors, equally detested, were looking their last on the city which they could not hold, and, inasmuch as the liberation of Jerusalem in 1917 will probably ameliorate the lot of the Jews more than that of any other community in Palestine, it was fitting that the flight of the Turks should have coincided with the national festival of the Hanukah, which commemorates the re-capture of the Temple from the heathen Seleucids by Judas Maccabæus in 165 B.C.

Chapter 15
After Jerusalem

During the last-mentioned operations, the Squadron had lost three officers and 67 men (out of the total of seven officers and 182 men, with which it started from Amr), and had only received one officer and three men as reinforcements. The losses in animals were: 50 riding horses, 15 draught and pack animals and one donkey. Of these animals, 25 had been killed at Tahta alone, and, considering that the Squadron had covered nearly 300 miles in five weeks, the losses due to fatigue, etc., were remarkably small. It was now necessary that the Squadron be re-equipped and re-organised, but reinforcements and remounts had first to be obtained, when training could be re-commenced.

At length on December 5th Sergt. Knowles and Sergt. Lewis, with 10 reinforcements, arrived from the base; Sergt. Knowles being posted to "D" Sub-section and Sergt. Lewis to "E". Both these Sergeants did excellent work. Unfortunately, Sergt. Lewis went to hospital shortly after he arrived, and was not able to return for a long time; owing to ill-health and bad luck, neither of them was able to go into action with the sub-sections they did so much towards making efficient.

A fortnight was spent at Akir in complete rest, after which the Brigade moved, via El Mughar and Beshshit, to the sand hills north-east of Esdud and about 1½ miles from the coast.

Conditions were not too pleasant here, but they might, perhaps, have been a great deal worse! The weather was very wet and cold and the sudden change from summer to winter was trying, even for the strongest constitutions. Being upon sand, the camp and district was certainly free from mud, but in order to water the horses a great sea of mud had to be gone through twice a day in order to reach the troughs that were erected at the Wadi Sukereir, two miles away. Warm clothing was issued out to all, and when fresh meat came up from the base, the members of the Squadron felt that they were enjoying luxury indeed!

December 21st brought a draft of 18 good fellows; the N.C.O.'s included Lance-Corpls. Gage, Laycock, Peach, Prior and Salter.

December 22nd saw the return of six old members of the Squadron who had gone to hospital during the last days of the "stunt," including Corpl. Franklin; he, however, had only been away a fortnight. Lieut. Millman and the personnel of "F" Section who went to Gamli from Amr, and afterwards to Belah, re-joined the Squadron at Esdud.

The Officer Commanding now grouped the Sub-sections together to form three sections. "No. 1" Section (consisting of "A" and "C" Sub-sections), under Lieut. Cazalet and Lieut. Oakley; "No. 2" Section ("B" and "D" Sub-sections) under Lieut. Hibbert and Sec.-Lieut. Kindell (now returned from hospital); "No. 3" Section ("E" and "F" Sub-sections) under Lieut. Millman ("F" Sub-section was still without horses). Sergt. Fleet, M.M., of "D" Sub-section had been promoted S.S.M., after S.S.M. Larwood had been wounded. Sergt. Knowles took his place in "D" on arrival. Reinforcements, and the Belah party, brought the five Sub-sections up to a reasonable strength: such was the position of affairs when Xmas drew near.

Everyone had been hoping to have *a real good time* this Christmas, to make up for the hardships endured through the "stunt". Puddings, beer and other good things, it was known, were on the way up, but, owing to difficulties with the bridge over the Wadi Ghuzze which interrupted railway traffic, when the day arrived, nothing had reached camp! The "goods" eventually turned up in time for the New Year but, there being a not very large percentage of Scotsmen in the Squadron, this did not make up for the disappointment at Xmas. Further, the weather on the day itself was certainly about the worst of the whole winter; blowing hard and raining incessantly, it was scarcely with a feeling of contentment that the men "turned in" that night—all doubtless thinking of brighter surroundings in the old country!

The first thing to happen in 1918 was a *move* to Belah; nights being spent at Medjel and Gaza on the way. The animals in the Brigade had not yet recovered from their previous exertions, and many a horse, unable to go further, had unfortunately to be led away and shot. Crossing the railway at Belah and turning to the west towards the fresh-water lake, the Brigade went round the north-end of the latter, right on to the low cliffs at the sea-shore, where the camp was to be located. There seemed to be promise of better times here than had been experienced at Esdud. The water for the horses was fairly close at hand and there was no mud.

The Brigade being now south of the bridge over the Wadi Ghuzze, rations were also likely to be better and the mail more regular; there was, in addition, a *canteen* at Belah!

Many changes in personnel took place about this time.

Before leaving Esdud S.Q.M.S. Harrison, Corpl. Barrett, Lance-Corpl. Blenkin, Ptes. Dransfield, F.W. Harrison, Ellams and Hadden left to become cadets in the R.A.F. Sergt. Fisher was promoted S.Q.M.S. Capt. Spencer, M.C., had arrived, being posted as second in command, but was re-posted a few days later, to the same position which he had previously held in the 18th Squadron. Capt. L.F. St. John Davies, M.C., arrived from the 21st Squadron the day Capt. Spencer left, and became second in command. Lieut. G.M. King was posted from the 17th Squadron (January 8th), and Sec.-Lieut. J.K.W. Arden arrived from the base (January 19th); Sec.-Lieut. Kindell was admitted to hospital again, but he returned within a few weeks.

Reinforcements continued to arrive, consisting of both old and new faces: January 6th, Lance.-Corpl. Keatley and six men; January 7th, Lance.-Corpl. G. Neal and 11 men; January 17th, Lance.-Corpl. Smith and 15 men; January 23rd, Saddler Hayward and eight men. Sec.-Lieut. Arden formed "F" Sub-section; remounts being now available. The Squadron thus became complete, having six Sub-sections. The training commenced, mounted drill, elementary gun drill, mechanism, "I.A.", special classes for range-finding, signalling, also lectures. N.C.O.'s were instructed in indirect fire. Lieut. Hibbert left for leave in the United Kingdom on February 10th, and Lieut. King took his place in "B" Sub-section, and O.C. "No. 2" Section.

On February 18th, Capt. D. Marshall, M.C., proceeded on leave to the United Kingdom, and Capt. L.F. St. John Davies, M.C., became O.C., with Lieut. Oakley second in command. On returning to the E.E.F. Capt. Marshall was posted to the 17th Squadron. On February 22nd the Brigade moved north to Gaza, or rather to about 1-1/2 miles south of it. Here there was a fair amount of graz-ing, and the animals were taken out every day for that purpose. They had been very slow in picking up condition, and it was hoped that this would do the necessary, as indeed it did.

The camp was arranged in the form of a square, a favourite formation with the Squadron, and a safe one during air raids. Water was a mile away in the Wadi Ghuzze, and rations were drawn from Gaza. On February 25th, Lieut. Oakley went to hospital; Lieut. King became second in command. On February 26th, Lieut. R.H. Fairbairns, M.C., arrived, and was posted to "No. 1" Section, taking command of "C" Sub-section. Training continued as at Belah, and on February 28th there was a Divisional Field Day—"crossing the Wadi Ghuzze," in which the 20th and 21st Squadrons were combined under Capt. R.O. Hutchinson, M.C., of the 21st.

On March 4th another Divisional Scheme took place on the hills south-east of the camp, the object being to intercept and defeat an imaginary enemy (represented in skeleton), advancing from Tel el Jemmi. This manoeuvre was satisfactorily performed.

On the 7th a pleasant diversion was made by a race meeting held by our neighbours, the 22nd Mounted Brigade. They had taken great trouble in preparing the course for both steeplechases and flat races, and on the day, a scene was presented very similar to a meeting at home, except for the absence of the ladies. On March 13th, Sec.-Lieut. J.W. Cummer arrived, and was posted to "C" Sub-section, Lieut. R.H. Fairbairns, M.C., being now second in command of the Squadron—a post which he held without interruption until he became Officer Commanding. On March 22nd, Sergt. Wright, who had been with the Squadron since its formation, left for an infantry cadet course at Zeitoun.

News was at this time received that H.R.H. The Duke of Connaught would shortly inspect our Brigade, which was now commanded by Brig.-Gen. G.V. Clarke, D.S.O.

At Belah: Officers, Warrant Officer & Sergeants

Several preliminary parades were, therefore, held, the inspection ultimately taking place on March 15th. After the march-past the Brigade was formed into a Square and H.R.H. expressed his high satisfaction with its appearance, and congratulated all ranks on their work of the previous year. After this speech he decorated the officers, N.C.O.'s and men, who had won distinction during the operations.

The 7th Brigade races were held on the 21st, and provided a good day's sport, but the engagement was rather spoiled by an almost continuous downpour of rain. Towards the end of March the "O.C." stated that he would shortly hold two test "turn-outs". At last, one morning, sub-sections were suddenly ordered to parade at once, in marching order by the troughs at the Wadi Ghuzze a mile away. "D" Sub-section was the first to arrive there, and the whole Squadron was at the rendezvous within 55 minutes—a most creditable performance!

The next "turn-out" was a practice "Air alarm". Ten guns were mounted outside the camp itself, all men took cover and the line-guards tripled in 1 minute 50 seconds!

A pleasant day's sport was provided by a friendly competition between the Squadron and the Field Ambulance— races, mounted sports, jumping, driving, etc.—and our Squadron proved successful in most of the events.

On April 1st, orders were received that the Brigade would move, the next day, back to the area previously occupied at Belah! They duly arrived, and the Machine-Gun Squadron took over identically the same camp as before, except that the "lines" were 100 yards further south. A few days after arriving here, rumours got around that several units were to be dismounted! Up till this time it was thought that this was the last thing that was likely to happen after their success in the last operations, and the knowledge of the country and open warfare that the troops had thereby gained. Unfortunately, the rumour proved to be only too true, and two regiments in each Brigade were ordered to hand over their

horses and proceed to the base. Here they underwent a
course of training for the Machine-Gun Corps, after which
they embarked for France, formed into Machine-Gun Battalions. The 7th Brigade having only two regiments, lost
only one—the South Notts Hussars, that being the junior.
At least two "graves" may be seen at Belah, each bearing
an inscription headed by "R.I.P." and a broken spur! Also
an "In Memoriam" to the lost horses of the South Notts
Hussars and the Warwick Yeomanry! The mock-ceremo-
nies, however, were carried out in all sincerity, as, who was
there who did not feel that he had lost a true friend, in being parted from his horse?

On April 7th, the 20th Squadron lent its horses to the Warwick Yeomanry to take them to the station, and on the 8th, to
the "S.N.H." for the same purpose. Ill-luck, however, attended
these regiments. After going through their course of training
they embarked at Alexandria, but they were no sooner out at
sea than their vessel was torpedoed and sunk! Many lives were
lost, including Lieut. Morris, who will be remembered by all
for his activities in the theatrical line, as, under his able direction, the "S.N.H. and the 20th Combined Concert Party"
provided us with a very excellent performance at Gaza.

Shortly after the departure of the "S.N.H.", the "S.R.Y."
were called upon to assist in an attack on the other side of
the Jordan. This operation was pushed right into the enemy
country, past Es Salt, which is the most difficult ground imaginable for cavalry, but, circumstances developing in an unexpected manner, a withdrawal had to be made. This movement was accomplished in a truly splendid fashion. The
affair, however, was not carried out without casualties, unfortunately, and the "S.R.Y." had to mourn the loss of Capt.
Layton, one of its most prominent Squadron leaders.

The absence of the "S.R.Y." left the 7th Mounted Brigade with only the B.H.Q. 20th M.G. Squadron, Essex Battery, Cav. F.A. and M.V.S. But it soon became known that

Indian Cavalry Regiments had arrived from France, and were to take the place of the regiments that had been dismounted for the M.G.C., and also to increase the number of cavalry in the country. An advance-party at length arrived in the Brigade, consisting of an officer from each regiment that was to join it, and these proved to be the "20th Deccan Horse" and "34th Poona Horse". Soon afterwards the regiments themselves arrived by train, with their horses. How these regiments would settle down in this country after their experience in France was at first a subject of interest to the Squadron. But the surroundings resembled, in some respects, their native India, and they were soon "at home". They only needed to forget the cramped warfare of the trenches in France and to practise real cavalry tactics again, to become a true part of the "E.E.F.". It was also evident, from the brightness of their steelwork, that they would be second to none in any ceremonial parade.

Training continued, and the Squadron was getting very efficient, both in the technical and tactical handling of guns. Barrage-drill (the latest introduction from Grantham), was practised, and an exhibition barrage, fired out to sea, proved very instructive. On April 18th, there was an "Action" competition for sub-sections under their respective Sergeants. They came into action at the gallop on targets at 400 yards range. "B" Sub-section was judged "best" with "A" Sub-section second.

Summer was rapidly approaching, and on May 15th "Reveille" had been altered to 04.45 to allow of the heat of the day being spent, as far as possible, in rest. An inter-unit sports competition, held with the Essex Battery, was exciting, and included a race on donkeys between the respective officers commanding! The total results gained were rather in favour of the Essex Battery.

During April a subscription list was opened for a Memorial to the fallen in the campaign, to be built in Jerusalem to which the Squadron subscribed £E14.

Sergt. Larwood, D.C.M., returned on April 11th, having quite recovered from the wound he received at Tahta. He was posted to "A" Sub-section. On the 21st Lieut. Cazalet was admitted to hospital.

During April Belah was considerably brightened, two large stationary hospitals being erected, to manage which a staff of nurses arrived! They certainly must have found Belah a quaint place after the civilised conditions to which they had been accustomed at Cairo and Alexandria, and in the course of their journey, as well as subsequently, they must have suffered many discomforts. Introductions, however, were hastily effected, and very soon, on afternoons, ladies could be seen out, riding with members of the British forces of the opposite sex.

Several ladies graced a concert given in the Squadron camp, being conducted there by certain gallants in two "G.S." wagons and "fours-in-hand"! Another diversion to the monotony here, was a trip to Jerusalem, which was well worth the tiring journey, although many were disappointed in the "side-show-at-an-exhibition" effect, which many of the most sacred spots presented. It was, however, gratifying to think, that this, the home of our religion, for which the Crusaders had fought and died, was at last rescued from the hands of the infidel. Ten days' leave was granted to Cairo, Port Said and Alexandria, but "turns" were necessarily very slow in coming round.

CHAPTER 16

Move to Sarona

The month of May heralded another "move," and at 09.00 on the 4th, the Brigade concentrated at the north end of Belah lake and set off northwards. Nights being spent, successively, three miles north-east of Gaza; two miles north-east of El Mejdel; one mile east of Wadi Sukereir (heavy downpour of rain on this day). On the 7th the trail led along the edge of the sand-dunes and through Yebna to Wadi Hanen. Here a halt of two hours was made, to water and feed. The country was very picturesque, being thickly planted with orange-groves, whilst here and there a red-tiled building was to be seen. At 13.00 the march was continued through Rishon-le-Zion to the main Jaffa-Ramleh road which is a thoroughly good metal one. Along this a few miles, thence north to Sarona, two miles north-east of Jaffa.

Arriving at Sarona at 16.30, the Squadron encamped beside an orange-grove and adjoining the Aerodrome. It may here be mentioned that Sarona before the war was a German colony, and from its appearance, must have been a prosperous one. The main street is lined on both sides with detached and semi-detached houses, mostly with red tiles, prettily designed. Fir trees are abundant and help to make a pleasing picture. Outside the village there are many orange-groves and vineyards, each with its red-tiled house, which has, either inside or in a separate building, a well with an engine for pumping water into a stone cistern, from which it is allowed to run, as required, along concrete gullies, and thus distributed over the land, irrigating it.

In consequence of the camp proving insanitary the morning after arrival, the Squadron moved about half a mile nearer the coast into a vineyard! This was an exceedingly pretty spot, from which an excellent view of Jaffa could be obtained; a few trees provided us with the unaccustomed luxury of some shade. The Brigade was attached to the 21st Infantry Corps and was "Corps Reserve". A training-area was allotted, and every morning the Squadron went out for mounted training through the village across the narrow gauge "Heath Robinson" railway, and through the orange-groves out to the area beyond Point 275 and north of the Village of Selmeh.

Capt. St. J. Davies, M.C., often gave each section a special task, or ordered them to concentrate at some place he might select from the map. Some of these little "stunts" were quite interesting, as often two sections would set off in almost opposite directions and yet they would arrive at the rendezvous at practically the same time!

On one of these occasions the horses were taken to the little River Auja[12] two miles north of the camp, and made to swim across, attached to an endless rope, being afterwards followed by the men.

On May 23rd the Brigade practised a "concentration" just north of the Auja and south-west of Sheik Muannis. Our Squadron did well! It arrived at the point three miles away, in full marching order within 40 minutes from the time the order was received. On May 28th, the Brigade moved forward north of the Auja, in reserve for the attack by the 7th Indian Division, but this movement was merely intended to capture a few enemy posts in order to narrow "no man's land," and thus bring ourselves into closer touch with the enemy. The Brigade remained "standing-by" at half an hour's notice until the evening of the 30th, when it returned to camp.

A Brigade scheme took place on June 7th, "No. 1" Section operated with the Poona Horse and one Squadron of "S.R.Y."; Nos. 2 and 3 Sections with the Deccan Horse and "S.R.Y." (less one squadron). On the 13th, another scheme was practised, "Defence of the Dahr Selmeh Ridge". A regimental scheme with the Poona Horse was also practised, besides several Squadron manoeuvres.

Sometimes the Squadron would go out before breakfast for the whole day, the usual routine of camp being carried on wherever they halted; returning "home" in the afternoon. One of these excursions brought the Squadron to the Jewish village of Mulebbis, where oranges could be bought by the cart-load. Two limbers were, therefore, taken back to camp fully loaded up; this was a discovery much appreciated by all, and two days later a fresh supply was sent for. Another local product bought at Jaffa and distilled at Rishon-le-Zion, was red wine. It was very good too! Bought by the Squadron canteen in large barrels, it was sold at 2½pt. (6d.) a pint.

The Squadron canteen was doing a good trade at this time. The N.A.C.B. at Jaffa kept a good stock, and Lance-Corpl. Prior rode down every day and bought large quantities of all kinds of provisions, as well as barrels of beer.

Jaffa, where the well-known Jaffa oranges are grown, is rather more like a European town than others in the country, but still is not to be compared in any respect with a British town of the same size. A very good Y.M.C.A. was established there, in which was a picture-house which provided welcome amusement in the evening. Daily bathing parades were instituted; the camp being barely a mile from the sea. The usual procedure was to ride to the shore and "link" horses. The men would then bathe and ride back. Quite half the horses were taken in the sea with the men, and they seemed to enjoy the sea just as much, after the first experience.

Reinforcements to the Squadron during May included Lieut. F.R. Wilgress (Lovats Scouts), who was posted to "A" Sub-section (and became Officer Commanding No. 1); Sergt. Lewis ("E" Sub-section), Lance-Corpls. Collett, Fuller and S.S. Fox.

As has been said, the camp, when it was first taken over, was a particularly pleasant one, but, as the summer advanced, flies became so numerous as to affect the health of the Squadron; the trees and bushes which at first had been looked on as an advantage, now provided excellent breeding places for the pests. South of Beersheba there are places where the ground is so thick with beetles that it is difficult to walk without treading on them at every step; at other places lizards are just as numerous, and they are as active as mice. In most parts of Palestine centipedes abound; these, if knocked off the skin in any other but the direction in which they are moving, are liable to cause a very bad inflammation and perhaps blood poisoning. Scorpions and tarantula spiders (which are just as poisonous); snakes which are deadly; sandflies, which cause a bad fever for several days; mosquitoes, which can inject malignant malarial germs capable of causing death in a few hours—these are a few of the many tortures. But of all these pests the common house fly, if in sufficient numbers, is a greater source of annoyance than any, besides being a spreader of disease. There certainly must have been millions upon millions of these flies, even within (say) 20 square yards!

Every effort was made to keep the flies down and "straffers" (a piece of wire gauze about three inches square provided with a handle) were issued. With these instru-

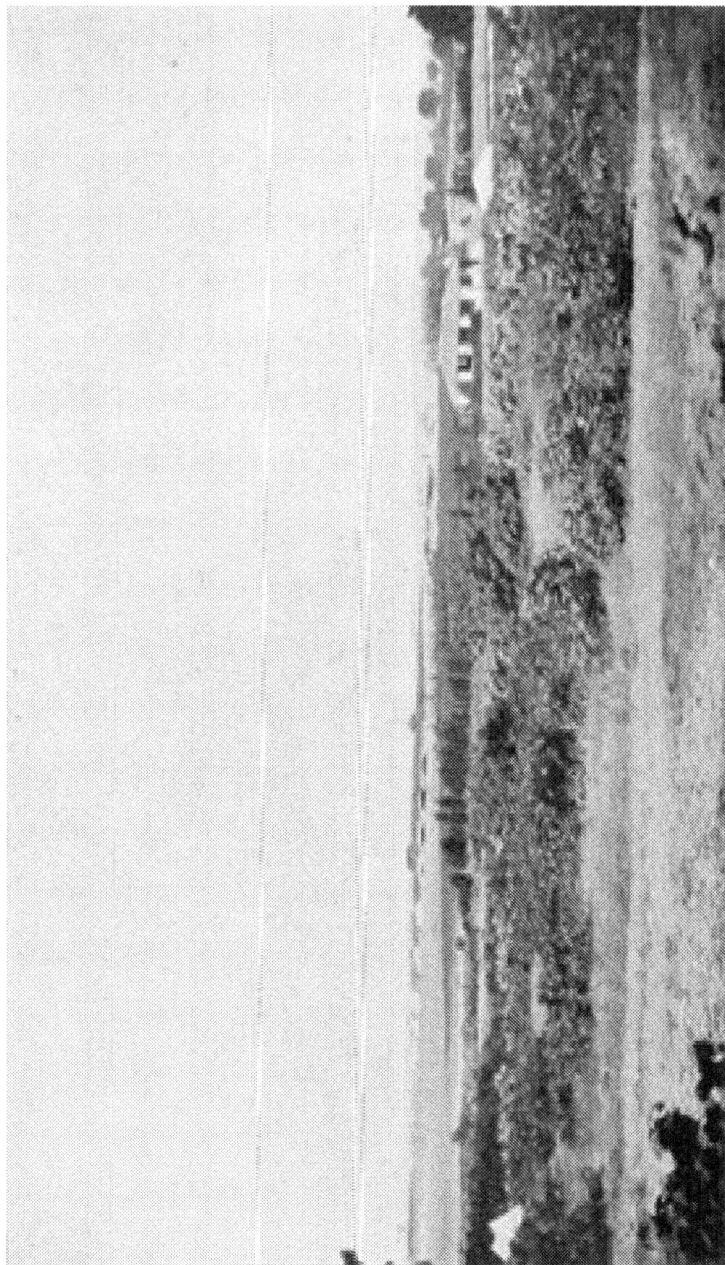

AT SARONA: A VIEW FROM OUR CAMP. R. A. F. HANGARS CAN BE SEEN IN THE DISTANCE

ments, the flies were killed as fast as the "straffers" could be brought down upon them. Medical officers inspected the camp and pronounced the sanitation excellent; yet the flies continued to flourish! The result of this fly-pest is seen in the number of men that were admitted to hospital from our Squadron: weeks ending May 10th, three; 17th, six; 24th, eight; 31st, three; June 7th, six; 14th, eight; 21st, nine; 28th, sixteen (including two officers, Lieut. Millman and Lieut. King); total 59, i.e. more than a quarter of the whole strength within eight weeks, and all for sickness, believed to be caused by flies!

As mentioned before, the Squadron camp overlooked the Aerodrome, and many fine exhibitions of flying were seen there. Boche planes paid us a visit occasionally, but that was only when none of ours were "up," and as soon as our men got moving he made off at top speed. Yet, the Boche brought off two coups that were, no doubt, pleasing to him! It should be mentioned that the British had one, sometimes two, observation balloons in this sector, from which the enemy's line, and the country behind it, could be seen very distinctly indeed, thus enabling our artillery to make it very unpleasant for any of the enemy's troops, not entrenched; the Turk, on the other hand, had no such opportunities. Our balloons, therefore, became special objects of the Turk's attention, and on two occasions, when he flew over to attack them, he was successful in bringing down on the first occasion two, and the second time one—in flames! Fortunately, the observers were all able to make their descent in parachutes! The Turk escaped, but only just in time—our machines were quickly on his "heels," and in spite of all his attentions, the following day found another British balloon in position just as if nothing had happened!

In consequence of the increased number of cavalry which had arrived in the country, the 7th Mounted Brigade now formed part of a Division, instead of being an independent Brigade, as heretofore. This Division, which was commanded by Major-Gen. H.J.M. MacAndrew, C.B., D.S.O., was at first styled the "2nd Mounted Division," but, later on, it was altered to the "5th Cavalry Division," comprising the 13th, 14th (the old 7th Mounted), and 15th (Imperial Service), Cavalry Brigades.

On June 27th, the Squadron paraded with the Brigade, in full marching order, for an inspection of the Division by the "C.-in-C.". They marched to the plain, north of Rishon-le-Zion, and were there duly inspected and "marched past," after which units returned to camp, independently. The "C.-in-C." expressed his high appreciation of the new Division. The next morning (June 28th 1918) a Divisional tactical scheme was carried out, and it was somewhat surprising to all ranks upon returning to camp, that orders were received for the Brigade to move that night at 01.00!

CHAPTER 17

Squadron Competitions

The Squadron, by this time, had made great progress in its training. It was, however, prevented from reaching that high state of efficiency which is always aimed at—owing to the constant change in its personnel, which was due to such numbers "going sick" to hospital.

A series of inter-sub-section competitions, however, was organised by the Officer Commanding, which were spread over a few weeks and proved very popular. The principal events were:

Detachment Competition in Marching Order: points being given for condition of animals and general turn-out—Won by No. 1 Detachment of E Sub-section, under Lance-Corpl. Smith.

Limber Competition—Won by D Sub-section (Drivers Harris and Collier, who also won a previous competition at Belah).

Action Competition, under Sub-section Sergeants: points given for— (1) Control—(A) Drill: (B) Led Horses: (C) Fire Orders, etc. (2) Time—taken from command Action to when led horses move back. (3) Gun Handling, Concealment and Shooting (won by D Sub-section, under Sergt. Pearse).

Belt Filling by Limber Drivers (won by C Sub-section).

Stripping, Adjustment, Minor Repairs and Immediate Action (1st,Lance-Corpl. Salter: 2nd, Lance-Corpl. Galway).

CHAPTER 18

March to the Jordan Valley

Before proceeding with a description of the Squadron's "trek" to the Jordan Valley, it might be desirable to enlighten the reader as to the actual position of affairs at the "front".

After the capture of Jerusalem on December 9th 1917, the Turk made one forlorn effort to re-capture it. This attempt met with not the slightest success, and afterwards (in February 1918), he was driven down into the Jordan Valley, where he had to yield up the town of Jericho to us. Since then (in March and April), two raids had been made into Turkish territory on the eastern side of the Jordan in the hills (in which the Sherwood Rangers Yeomanry, and Essex Battery R.H.A. participated), and on each occasion, the towns of Es-Salt and Amman were reached. A large number of prisoners were taken, together with machine-guns and ammunition, added to which several bridges were destroyed, and the Hedjaz railway from Damascus to Mecca cut, thus endangering the Turkish troops, which were operating against the Arab Sherifian Army, further south. Elsewhere on the front, the position of the "line" had not materially changed, and at the time of the 20th Machine-Gun Squadron's tour of duty in the Jordan Valley, it extended from the coast north of Jaffa south-eastwards across country (through a point 18 miles north of Jerusalem), to the Jordan Valley, thence, due south along the eastern bank of the river to the Dead Sea.

Now, it will be readily imagined that when a unit has remained for any length of time in one place it has automatically collected large quantities of stores, equipment, etc., which naturally cannot be carried, when on the march. On this occasion the principal difficulty lay in the stock of "canteen goods" that we had accumulated. Fortunately the "R.A.F." came to the rescue and bought the whole lot, "lock, stock and barrel".

As has been stated, there was much sickness in the Squadron at this time, but many men were able to keep themselves out of hospital because of the fact that the Squadron was "at rest," besides, they preferred to rough it, rather than leave their duties. A "sick-parade" was now hurriedly called in order to dispose of those who could not be expected to take part in the next "trek". This parade, however, was vetoed from the start, and was, in fact, unpopular. Only two men turned up! These, with the two officers previously mentioned (all of whom ought to have "gone down the line" several days before), were accordingly sent to hospital. Many men were suffering from septic sores on their legs and feet; permission was asked (and granted), for these cases, to wear "slacks" or shoes, as might be necessary. Strange as it might seem, these men preferred to suffer and remain with the Squadron, when there seemed a chance that they might be able to come to grips with the enemy and do something really useful.

In these circumstances, it was not a very smart Squadron that paraded that night, but its spirit would require a lot of beating! The route lay past Yazur, on the Jaffa road, to Ramleh, which town they were approaching as day broke, and Ludd could also be seen. The latter town will be remembered by all who had occasion to go to Egypt for leave or to take a course of instruction, also by reinforcements who joined the Squadron about this time, as it was the British railhead; the journey from here to Kantara on the Suez Canal being accomplished overnight. From Ludd, also, there is a branch line to Jerusalem, and a narrow gauge railway to Sarona. At Ramleh, turning off the road to the right, and passing Lieut. Price's grave, we halted, off-saddled, watered and fed. At 14.00 a further march, arriving at the water troughs east of Latron at 17.00, camping for the night further up the road. Fairly on the way to the famous Jordan Valley, ill-accounts of which they had often heard, we were soon to find that these reports had not been at all exaggerated!

The next morning (June 30th), the road in front being very steep, rising continually, with often a drop of several hundred feet on either side, units started at half-hour intervals.

The necessity of this soon became evident. The road was crowded with motors of all kinds, and it was by no means a joke to ride a restive horse while leading an obstinate mule, along the brink of a precipice! At 13.00 Enab was reached, where the Squadron was allotted its ground, rather stony, but next to the water troughs, which, however, saved a lot of work.

The following afternoon (July 1st), the road being steeper still, the transport ("A" Echelon), went ahead of the Brigade. The Squadron started at 14.30 (units still moving at half-hour intervals), and proceeded along the main Jerusalem road through the new town, past the Damascus Gate (at 17.30), to the eastern side of the town, where the transport was passed and the Brigade concentrated, the highest point having now been reached (2,590 feet above sea level). A halt of two hours was made, and at 20.00 the descent to the Jordan was commenced. Henceforth it was "down," "down," all the way, with roads just as precipitous as before, but the mountains being so high and steep on both sides, not a breath of air reached us. At 02.30 after a tiring march, and after passing the "Inn of the Good Samaritan," we arrived at the water troughs at Talat-ed-Dumm (1,018 feet above sea level). After watering, about half an hour later, the Squadron found its camping ground, a space barely large enough for a section. In this cramped area the whole of the Squadron was crammed "as tight as sardines in a tin," with, literally, not an inch to spare!

Early next morning, when the sun began to rise, some idea was gained of what might be expected in the Jordan Valley. Although Talat-ed-Dumm, as already stated, is 1,018 feet above the level of the sea, shut in, as it is, among the mountains away from any breeze, the heat there is almost unbearable; the rays of the sun seem to take on a hundred times more power than ever could be believed possible, blazing down from right overhead, and leaving no shade, thus turning the place into a veritable furnace.

The Brigade did not continue the march again until 19.00, when it moved along the old Roman road. Still "down," "down," round sharp bends, and still along the edges of precipices hundreds of feet deep! At length a final, particularly steep slope, brought us to Jericho, on the plain of the Jordan Valley, and 820 feet below the level of the sea. A halt was made here for a short time, and then the Brigade marched north-east (through clouds of dust), to its camping area in the Wadi Nueiame, arriving at midnight. Here, on dismounting in the dark, one seemed to be standing in mud, but, upon closer examination, this was found to be merely several inches of fine dust! Sec.-Lieut. Cummer, whose turn it was to be with the advance party that day, was waiting to show the Squadron its camping ground, which turned out to be as good as could be expected, and alongside a stream. A few bell-tents were already standing, which were appreciated.

The following are a few extracts from the notes of a member of the Squadron, which gives a vivid description of his experiences on the road to the Jordan. He says:

The sun was just setting as we approached Jerusalem, and the ancient walls of the Holy City were bathed in orange light against an opalescent sky. The long dusty column of the Brigade toiled its way up the steep hill into the city, and passing close by the Jaffa Gate 'turned left' and followed the main thoroughfare towards the Damascus Gate. Outside of Fast's Hotel (a former German concern, but now famous throughout the E.E.F.) stands a group of officers and soldiers, watching our brigade pass, and cheering us on as we move into the dusk.

Over the Mount of Olives, past the Garden of Gethsemane (the black points of its many cypress trees now silhouetted against the sky), what thoughts are ours as we cross this hallowed ground amid surroundings so deeply associated with our religion! Some of us may never return, but yet we shall have followed to our fate along a path that still holds memories of that greatest sacrifice the world has ever known!

Dark has fallen, and the stars shine bright in a velvet sky. At length we approach the little Village of Bethany, 'the town of Mary and Martha'; near which we dismount and breathe our horses for a space; finding a little shop close at hand, we buy some fruit and 'take a pull' at the water-bottle.

Leaving our last link with civilization we begin our long weary descent to the Jordan Valley. Before we have covered a mile, it is obvious that the road is falling steeply. 'Take a good breath now of the fresh air,' say those who have already experienced the Jordan Valley, 'for it's the last you'll get for many a day!'

The road now enters a valley, or more rightly passes between two lines of rocky hills, and for a time, as it is pitch dark, we stumble along to keep our places in the column. But soon, the eastern crest is silhouetted by the rising moon, and as the silver light pours down the slope we see the road before us, zig-zagging its way 'into the depths,' and there, a mile in front, the head of the Brigade worming its way, like a great black snake.

So steep is it now, and so sharp the 'hairpin' turns, that although one hears the voices and sees the heads of troops on the winding road forty yards below, yet these are possibly half a mile ahead in the column! 'Down' and 'down' we go, hotter and hotter it grows, dustier and dustier the atmosphere!

Great difficulty is now experienced in keeping touch with the regiment in front, for in such cases it is always the Machine-Gun Squadron that is in rear of the column and 'enjoys' the dust. In action or danger—quite another thing; up, then, just behind the leading regiment....

Arrived at Talat-ed-Dumm, too tired now to eat or drink (having fed our animals) we lie, or rather, fall down on a blanket. In two minutes we are dreaming that we are back in the 'old country,' sitting in that cool breeze under the great sycamore tree; drinking that fine old 'home-brewed,' and talking to the sweetest of all women. Far away in the distance is the rumbling of a coach; round the corner it comes into sight, the horses' hoofs thudding on the hard old Roman road! The guard raises his long coaching horn to his lips and blows a stirring call. Someone shakes us from behind! Lo! we open our eyes and—gone is the lovely green country, the shady trees and the coach! 'Get up! Reveille has gone'.

All day we rest here, and shall move on the latter part of our 25-mile journey as soon as dark has fallen. Horses to water—but luckily not far to go, and though two men have fainted with the heat already, the majority are still 'merry and bright'.

About 11 o'clock Talat-ed-Dumm becomes literally an oven; no trees, no water, nothing but rock and dust—dust six inches deep; the only protection, a single piece of canvas between one and the pitiless sun! Gasping for breath, one reaches for the water-bottle, but it is quite warm. Still, a warm drink brings perspiration, and that is cooling to a certain extent—in its after-effects!

Night falls, welcomely, and saddled up the Squadron waits for the advance to begin and to drop into its place in the line of march as the Brigade moves past. Voices in the darkness, then shadowy forms, and, their horses' hoofs muffled by the dust, Brigade Headquarters passes by. Then the three regiments, one British and two Indian, each of the latter followed by crowds of donkeys looking ghostly white in the gloom. At length it is our turn, and behind the last regiment we 'walk march' and once more get the clouds of dust for our portion. Now, along the level for a time—and then down again, down towards the valley, to many a valley of death!

The impression we get, on leaving Talat-ed-Dumm, is rather different from that ascribed to tourists in the guide book to Palestine. 'It is with regret,' it says, 'that we drag ourselves away from a spot of such historic interest, where so many of the patriarchs have rested'. God help 'em! we never wish to see it again. No wonder to us, now, that Naaman the Syrian objected to go down to the Jordan and wash seven times in it!

The horses slip and slide as they pick their way down the old Turkish road, and once more the moon looks over the hills and floods her silvery radiance over all—the same moon that in two hours will rise upon the old homestead in Blighty. But here are we, among great mountains, rugged and cleft, fantastic shapes in high relief, in the moonlight. We might be in the moon itself! Not a sign of life, not a bird nor an animal!

By mid-night we have dropped 1,100 feet, and gradually the ground grows less rocky, the hills on the right swing away, and on the left, just ahead, is the square-topped El-Kuruntal, the so-called 'Mountain of Temptation,' and the gateway of the Jordan Valley. Reaching the plain the pace grows faster, and clouds of dust arise worse than ever. Our connecting files find great difficulty in keeping in touch, so that every now and then those in rear must gallop to keep up. A small wadi to be crossed makes the pace still more uneven. We cross the Wadi Nueiame and reach our camping ground. Again the putting down of lines; again supperless and tired

out to lie down on a blanket in the dust, in that un-
natural hollow 1,250 feet below the sea-level, the place
of sweltering sun, sand-spouts, scorpions, snakes, spiders and septic sores; of scorching wind and shadowless
waste; that hellish place—the jordan valley!

CHAPTER 19

The Jordan Valley Campaign

A few days were necessarily spent in the Wadi Nueiame in exercising the horses and becoming acclimatized to the temperature, which rarely falls below 100°, even at night, and is usually 120° in the shade (or over) during the day. On July 7th, "No. 1" Section paraded at 19.00 and proceeded to the east of the Jordan to relieve a section of the 21st Squadron in the line. "A" Sub-section took over the emplacements in No. 3 Post, and "C" Sub-section those in No. 5 Post. The relief was completed by 23.00. The next evening, the remainder of the Squadron relieved the 21st Squadron in their camp at the Ghoraniyeh Bridge. One section only going at a time to avoid attracting attention and being shelled by the Turks, who were posted in the hills. The new camp was within 100 yards of the Jordan,[18] nearly surrounded by cliffs, the tops of which were level with the plain above. The cliffs themselves only being formed by the depression in the plain before it gives way to the lower ground in the immediate vicinity of the River Jordan and the east of it. The river at this point is actually 1,250 feet below the level of the sea!

On arriving in the camp, "No. 2" Section took over

the machine-gun positions for the inner defences of the bridgehead. These had to be manned at night only, and were on the tops of the cliffs near the camp, commanding all the crossings of the river. Every evening just before dusk (sometimes in a severe dust storm), the four guns were taken up on the pack-mules by the gun-teams and brought back after light the next morning. "No. 3" Section was in Divisional reserve, and liable to be called on at short notice to proceed to any part of the line. It provided also all the camp fatigues.

It was soon found that summer-life in the Jordan Valley was about the limit of discomfort; only those who have been there at that season can have any idea of what it is like. If only our turn had been in the winter, when according to all accounts the weather is bearable! Needless to say that as much work as possible was done in the early morning and evening, but even this was extremely trying for all. Fortunately, water was available from a small stream just outside the camp. Rush-huts and bivouacs provided the best protection against the sun. Material for these was obtained from the banks of the Jordan, where, for a few yards on either side, there was luxurious vegetation—in striking contrast with the rest of the country; during the day men were allowed to bathe in the river.

All wheels had to be covered over during the day in order to prevent the wood shrinking; if this had not been done, very little transport could have been brought out of the valley at the end of the Brigade's tour of duty!

There is, a little over a mile east of the Jordan, a series of low isolated hills; upon these was situated our line of defence. Each hill, fortified with barbed-wire and trenches, constituted a "post". This line was held by Indian Infantry, the regiments of the cavalry brigade providing the patrols in "no man's land," which, several miles wide, was intersected by thousands of wadis (providing excellent cover

SQUADRON CAMP IN YHE JORDAN VALLEY: NO. 2 SECTION

for a stealthy enemy), also a certain amount of tall grass.

The enemy's position was on the mountains at the eastern side of the Jordan Valley, completely overlooking ours. Earlier in the year they had crossed the intervening ground, under cover of darkness, and attempted to send us to "Jericho". They had found the posts too strong for them, however, and had retired to the positions now mentioned.

"C" Sub-section was on the left, on the banks of the Wadi Nimrin—a broad wadi with a small stream running along its centre. This wadi ran right from the Turkish positions to the Jordan near the Squadron camp. "A" Sub-section was about half a mile away to the right in the centre of a cluster of small hills. "A's" horses were between the two Sub-sections, and "C's" were a few hundred yards behind its position under a cliff beside the Nimrin. If anything, it was probably more pleasant to be with the sections in the line than in the Squadron Camp.

Nothing of importance happened during our first week. Shells came over every day at unexpected moments in odd places, and Boche planes paid regular visits, dropping bombs, always, however, receiving a bombardment from our "Archies". But on the morning of July 14th, after a night of more than the usual amount of artillery fire, shells began to fall all around, not to mention the shrapnel exploding overhead; this state of affairs continued throughout the whole morning. "No. 2" Section in camp was well protected by a high cliff, but "No. 3" was not so fortunate and had to be moved. All the horses had been taken to another spot, and Sergt. Lewis with some men were seeing that everything required had been removed, when a shell pitched right in the centre of the "lines" and wounded him and Ptes. H. Reed and L. Peach. All the day the shelling continued; the immediate neighbourhood of the bridges over the Jordan being the "warmest" spot. A field ambulance, close to the Squadron, behind the right reserve gun position, suffered badly. In the evening all shelling stopped—more suddenly even than it had started!

Afterwards was learnt the cause of the excitement. The Turk, it was ascertained, had intended an attack all along the line. At one point, only, had the movement matured, and this was opposite the Australian Section, on our left. Here, German troops succeeded in getting right round some of the posts and endangering our bridgehead defences; they had moved guns up, which enabled them to reach places previously out of range of anything but their "heavies". Although surrounded, the posts named still held out, and the Boches were finally driven back to their starting point, where, it is said, they were fired on by the Turks!

On July 17th, "No. 2" Section relieved "No. 1" in the line. "No. 3" took over the inner defences, and "No. 1" became Divisional reserve. Lieut. E.B. Hibbert (who left in February 1918 for leave and a course in the United Kingdom) returned on July 25th and took command of "No. 3" Section. On August 3rd "No. 3" Section relieved "No. 2", the inner defences being taken over by "No. 1". A few days later "No. 3" Section was withdrawn from the posts and camped close to Brigade Headquarters to be employed as Mobile Reserve for the outer defences, but owing to shortage of personnel in the posts, the guns had to be mounted in their previous positions at night.

The "Valley" soon began to affect the health of the Squadron. All kinds of fever became rampant, particularly malaria. Men would suddenly become sick, or collapse in a fainting fit, their temperature quickly rising to 104° or thereabouts! Doctors and medical orderlies were much overworked, and became almost unable to cope with the "rush"; men had to be undressed and tended on the spot by their own comrades, who sponged them down in order to reduce their temperature. The Squadron's thanks are due to Pte. Ineson, who, as its own medical orderly, was untiring in his attention to the sick. Undoubtedly, but for his efforts, the list of men admitted to hospital would have been considerably larger.

During July, the O.C. (Capt. L.F. St. J. Davies, M.C., who soon returned, however, although not quite recovered), and 38 men, were admitted to hospital. On August 10th, Lieut. Wilgress and Lieut. Hibbert went to hospital.

When the Squadron left the Valley on August 15th (being relieved by the 21st Squadron), the total casualties were three officers and 113 O.R.'s. Fortunately, a number of reinforcements had arrived, including many from Yeomanry regiments recently dismounted. The first halt was Talat-ed-Dumm, where the 17th Squadron was passed at 02.30 on its way down to the valley. A better camping site was available than the last time, when we camped here.

The following evening the march was continued, and Jerusalem was passed through at midnight. The next morning the Brigade arrived at Enaɔ, having watered at the troughs at Ain el Foka, on the way. The same evening the Brigade moved via Latron, Barriyeh and Naane to Khurbet Deiran arriving at 07.30 the next morning, the rest of the day being spent in laying out the new camp. That day Lieut. Cazalet returned from hospital and temporarily took command of "No. 2" Section (while Lieut. Kindell went on a course at Zeitoun), afterwards taking over his old section ("No. 1").

No sooner had the Brigade settled down in its new quarters than very strenuous training was re-commenced—in addition there were inspections galore—besides tactical schemes, almost every other day. Reinforcements came up, which included many men new to the Squadron, which was, in consequence, soon nearly up to strength. Lieut. King returned from hospital, but still being far from well had, soon afterwards, to go back there. On September 13th Lieut. Millman returned from hospital and Lieut. Kindell from his course of instruction. Lieut. Millman resumed command of his late section ("No. 3"). On September 14th the Squadron turned out in complete marching order with transport, for a Divisional "scheme," the Division moving south on a six-mile frontage, sections coming into action with an imaginary enemy at various points.

CHAPTER 20

The Great Advance of 1918

So well had the secret of the great operations, that were in view by the Commander-in-Chief, been kept, that no one in the Squadron had any idea of a general attack being in contemplation. It was, in fact, not until the day that the Squadron was ordered to strike camp, that any officer or man (except perhaps the officer commanding), became aware that a serious movement was about to take place! An attack at any time would not, of course, have been entirely unexpected, as we were always prepared for something of the kind, but on this occasion the rumours that usually precede operations of importance were entirely absent—although the number of tactical schemes recently practised should have indicated that some particular purpose was in view.

At 18.00 on September 17th, the Squadron paraded in full marching order, and moved off, leaving all tents and buildings standing. We never returned to those quarters!

The strength of the Squadron at this time was six officers, 212 O.R.'s, 181 riding horses, 80 draft mules, 43 pack animals. So far as can be ascertained now, the following were the officers and N.C.O.'s:

Headquarters: Major L.F. St. John Davies, M.C. Capt. R.H. Fairbairns, M.C. S.S.M. Fleet, M.M. S.Q.M.S. Fisher. Farr.-Staff-Sergt. Robertson. Sergt. Conuel (Transport). Sergt. Ramsay (Orderly Room). S.S.-Corpl. Anderson. Sig.-Corpl. Foster. Saddler-Corpl. Mellett.

"No. 1" Section:

Sec-Lieut. J.W. Cummer.

"A" Sub-section:	"C" Sub-section:
Sergt. Larwood, D.C.M.	Sergt. Roberts
Corpl. Rouse	Corpl. Gage
Lance-Corpl. Holt	Lance-Corpl. Rose
Lance-Corpl. Moverley	Lance-Corpl. Sneddon

"No. 2" Section:

Lieut. A.O.W. Kindell.

"B" Sub-section:	"D" Sub-section:
Sergt. Hazlehurst	Sergt. Salter
Corpl. Rouse	Corpl. Gage
Lance-Corpl. Lawson	Lance-Corpl. Fox
Lance-Corpl. Stokes	Lance-Corpl. Fuller
Corpl.Pearse	

"No. 3" Section:

Lieut. A.G.P. Millman; Sec.-Lieut. J.K.W. Arden.

"E" Sub-section:	"F" Sub-section:
Sergt. Potts	Sergt. Grice, M. M.
Corpl. Thompson	Corpl. Keetley
Lance-Corpl. Lawson	Lance-Corpl. Fox
Lance-Corpl. Pountain	Lance-Corpl. Buckingham
Lance-Corpl. Woodhouse	Lance-Corpl. Patterson

The route taken was familiar to everyone. Passing Rishon-le-Zion (Ayun Kara) the Squadron came upon its old friend the Jaffa Road, thence, past Yazur to Sarona, by exactly the same way as was taken in the previous May. Bearing to the left, past the village, we arrived at Summeil and the camp south of the River Auja, where Sec.-Lieut. Arden, who had been sent on in advance to take over the Squadron area, showed us our position in the camp. Arriving at dusk the whole Brigade (horses, wagons and men), were hidden in orange groves; it was certainly not an easy task to fit everything up in the dark, the avenues between the trees being narrow and in most places only allowing horses to be led in single file.

The orders for the morrow (equally unenlightening) were to the effect that no unnecessary movement was to take place, and that no one, on any account, was to go outside the groves; the horses were to be watered at stated hours from the stone gullies used by the natives for the irrigation of the plantations; no fires were allowed; and all cooking was to be done with the methylated spirit blocks which were issued out for the purpose.

The daytime was passed without incident, but 18.30 found the Brigade paraded outside the groves ready to march at dusk. Crossing the Auja by the wooden bridge, and proceeding stealthily along the sea shore, below the cliffs, about five miles to west of El Jelil, it halted in "column of troops," off-saddled, watered from a trough, supplied by water from a well dug beside it, "linked" horses and laid down on the sand to get some sleep. It may be imagined that by this time everyone was wondering what the next day would bring forth!

Before daylight we were saddled up and "standing to"— a vigorous bombardment of the Turkish trenches (which we had been told the previous night to expect) was in full swing. Suddenly, it stopped! Who was there among us who did not think of the part the infantry were then playing, and upon whose successful attack so much was to depend?

When would orders arrive for us, on the beach, to move? Patiently waiting and expecting, nothing however came! Suddenly at 07.00, the troops in front were seen mounting, and at length the surprising order came through to us that the entire Division was to make its way to Nazareth—quite 50 miles behind the enemy's line, as the crow flies!

The 13th Brigade, being on the sands in front of the 14th, was to lead this movement. The Poona Horse were to be the leading regiment of the 14th, with ourselves (the 20th Machine-Gun Squadron) immediately behind them.

Upon advancing a short way up the coast, we reached what had been the British front line, and evidences of the morning's action were to be seen, as here and there several dead men and mules were lying about. As we passed by this spot, an officer of an Infantry Machine-Gun Company called out to us: "Good luck, get us back our guns. They raided us this morning and captured two!"

A few yards further on, the old Turkish line was reached and a number of killed and wounded Turks and animals were to be seen here also.

Right along the coast we went, "without let or hindrance," the high cliffs affording us protection from the few shells coming over, nearly all of which fell into the sea. The pace was killing, and the sand and rocks made it heavy going for the horses. They were very fit though, thanks to the hard training they had had at Deiran!

Still proceeding northward, about six miles along the coast, the cliffs suddenly gave way to flatter ground; here we turned inland in a north-easterly direction. Reports reached us that about 200 enemy infantry (with transport) were in a wood on our right flank. "No. 1" Section and one squadron of Poona Horse were detailed as "flank guard" to prevent the enemy leaving the wood until the Brigade had passed by. The flank guard, however, were instructed not to trouble to dispose of this small party, as bigger "fish" were in view.

At 11.30 the Brigade had reached the Nahr Iskanderun. After crossing slowly by two small, very shaky, bridges, units hurriedly watered here, independently, by means of buckets, the banks of the stream being very steep. The country now became delightful, cultivated, everywhere, with orange groves and gardens. At 12.30 the Brigade, winding its way through the groves, came out into the pretty little Village of Liktera (a Jewish settlement called by them Hudeira), 26 miles from the starting point. The inhabitants were overjoyed to see us, and as a halt was made here, and horses off-saddled and fed, they soon made us at home with gifts of bread, eggs and milk, refusing to take any payment therefor.

Until the inhabitants had seen the head of our Division, about a mile off, they had not the slightest idea that there had even been a British attack! They were particularly anxious to know how the people were faring in such villages as Mulebbis, and other places, south of our old line, where they had friends and relatives. As indicative that our advance was carried out with speed and secrecy—while we were resting here, a Boche motor lorry arrived! The driver, being unaware of anything unusual, drove quietly into the town; he nearly fell off his seat when he was suddenly surrounded by British troops! This lorry proved to be the advance guard of several more, all of which were, of course, captured.

CHAPTER 21

Capture of El Fule

After a sleep in the afternoon (what a luxury for the first day of a "stunt!") and tea, the Brigade saddled up and moved off at 18.00, just before dark. What a cheery crowd it was! But they had "some" march in front of them, the object being the capture of Nazareth and the cutting of the Turk's principal line of communication, which would isolate practically the whole of his army west of the Jordan! Just outside the village, two large marquees—a German Field Ambulance—hurriedly evacuated, were passed. Earlier in the day an officer of the 13th Brigade had found an untasted breakfast here, for which he had much reason to be thankful!

Further on, the track taken (the main route being avoided) proved very bad, and in many places the whole division had to proceed in "single file". In some places, also, horses were led. The natives, who had gathered upon the road-side from the villages which we passed, stood silently watching us. They must have been amazed, and the troops must have appeared to them veritable "ghosts of the night". At 23.30 a halt of 30 minutes was made, at a small village, and horses fed. In the early hours of the morning many horses, belonging to the forward part of the column, were passed by the wayside. They were completely "done". No doubt they were, in some cases, able, later on, to join up, but in their present state their riders had taken their saddles off and had lain down beside them, to sleep. For the moment these men had nothing further to do, but they must have run a serious risk from hostile natives when the Brigade had passed by. At 04.00 the next morning we emerged upon the open Plain of Esdraelon.

Now was to take place an interesting development in the operations. With Nazareth within fairly close reach, our objective was at hand. We formed up as quickly as possible in "Line of troop column," and then moved along the plain to the east, heading slightly towards the north, gradually nearing the north side as we proceeded forward. The objective for the 14th Brigade was to cut the main road to Nazareth from the south, thus cutting off all communication between the Turkish General Headquarters at Nazareth and their line, which ran across the country from Arsuf to the north of the Dead Sea. The 13th Brigade, which, it will be remembered, up to this point had been the leading one, after forming up, made for the hills on the other side of the plain, and, reaching them, turned to the east, towards their objective which was the Turkish General Headquarters at Nazareth!

The "going" on the plain was very bad, especially in the dark, the ground being a network of cracks and covered with a species of tall needle-grass, the latter making it very painful for the horses, whilst the former, continually giving way under their weight made the risk of broken legs a real one. Fortunately, however, no serious accidents took place. What wonderful creatures horses are! Those who were on that trek could not fail to realise it, if they had never done so before! As time went on and the goal was still not reached, it seemed that they must drop at any minute, but still they kept on, never faltering! A few dropped out, it is true, but they were a very small percentage of the whole. What courage and endurance they showed, to carry a weight of (say) 18 stone, 50 miles in 24 hours over the worst country imaginable!

About half way across the plain, the railway to Haifa was "cut," and, pushing on, there were still some miles to go when day began to break. Many thought they would now be "in for" a hot time, and expected guns to open upon them from all sides.

But the Turk was still quite ignorant of our presence. In any case he was not prepared for an attack at that distance behind his line! When it became fully light the 13th Brigade could be seen on the top of the ridge on the left moving parallel with us, and, in front of us, there was Mount Tabor which served as a "guide" for direction. At 05.30 enemy motor lorries were seen crossing our front going towards Nazareth. We opened fire upon them but they did not stop.

Proceeding up the hill, they discovered that our 13th Brigade troops were on the top, when they stopped about half way up and opened fire with machine-guns. Upon this our "No. 2" Section came up and "peppered" them. One lorry caught fire and after a short time the occupants of the convoy, trying to escape up the hill, were captured by the 13th Brigade. Shortly after this incident, Turkish troops were seen marching up the road towards us, but a squadron from the Sherwood Rangers and Deccan Horse with our "No. 3" Section quickly caused them to be quite in a hurry to surrender. From a small rise could be seen, looking down the road, a large camp and El Fule railway station with trucks, carriages and engines, also large dumps of material. Everywhere, crowds of enemy troops were to be seen rushing about; apparently in a state of great panic. In these circumstances a squadron of the Deccan Horse went down to "look into things" and after "dealing" with a few of the excitable "Johnnies" the remainder surrendered.

About 900 prisoners were taken that morning. Later on in the day the Brigade moved down to the station and encamped, the horses being watered from a trough which was discovered about a mile along the railway.

Here, there was found a large quantity of stores of all descriptions, including Turkish cigarettes, which were not refused as a ration on such an occasion. The capture of El Fule released an R.A.F. pilot, who, having to land in consequence of engine trouble that morning, had been taken prisoner by some Austrian gunners who, with their horses only, were retreating. They were anxious to know which way the British were coming, in order to decide which road they should take. Of course they did not learn anything, but fortunately came along this road and thus fell into our hands.

Here it might be mentioned that the work of the R.A.F. was truly wonderful. Prior to the "stunt," in order to ensure that the enemy should not be aware of the massing of our cavalry just before the attack and their subsequent movements after the infantry had broken through, they flew continually over the enemy aerodromes and prevented enemy airmen from rising. Perhaps it should be said they rather tempted them to do so, but—they never did! Consequently, on the day of our attack, the enemy had no information at all of what was happening, as his planes were on the ground and remained there until they were either burnt or captured. They certainly would not rise! At El Fule a very large aerodrome had been established, and a large collection of enemy machines was found there. It was not long before these were joined by some of our own which arrived almost as soon as it had been taken.

During the day the 13th Brigade had been dealing with Nazareth, and that night our Brigade slept at El Fule. Next morning we were to go southwards to Jenin (which might or might not have been captured), and clear the intervening country.

With this end somewhat in view, Lieut. Kindell was ordered to fix up two machine-guns in a captured Boche motor-car, and, acting as left "flank guard" to the Brigade, was directed to go to Jenin by a road running parallel to, and on the left of, the one to be taken by the Brigade. When fitted up the car looked quite formidable. Lance-Corpls. Fox and Fuller and Ptes. Boak (with signal flags) and Franklin accompanied him. The driver of the Brigade car was lent for this special occasion.

After re-filling with German petrol in the morning, they started off upon their journey. They soon came up with all kinds of derelict enemy transport and Turkish stragglers coming in. At one point ahead, could be seen a crowd of people (which proved to be natives) around some deserted enemy motor lorries. A troop of "S.R.Y." (detached from the Brigade for the purpose), came galloping over, but, as already stated, they proved to be only villagers looking about for some "plunder," and they were soon sent about their business. Further on Lieut. Kindell's car was joined by two other cars of the "Light Car Patrol" each with a machine-gun, so that the party now consisted of three cars with four guns.

On arriving at Jenin they found the streets simply choked with abandoned Turkish transport. It was only by moving each wagon aside by hand that they were able to proceed through the town and meet the Brigade before it arrived there on the other side; the cars were then sent off again on a patrol. Unfortunately, upon returning through the town, the driver of our car, on turning a corner, ran into the pole of a wagon, and broke the radiator. Such was the end of the Squadron "armoured" car, much to the disappointment of the occupants, who were just beginning to enjoy their novel experience.

It should be stated that the town of Jenin, together with a very large number of prisoners, had been captured the previous night by the Australians. Here, too, was an aero-drome and several burnt enemy planes—more evidence of the splendid work of the R.A.F.

Our Brigade remained in the Jenin area until evening, when, having watered, we went back along the El Fule road towards Nazareth and about half way, bore off to the right, encamping upon the hills south-east of El Fule and south of the El Fule-Beisan Road. The next morning (22nd September), we moved down the hills northwards and camped just south of the Beisan Road, near water. The day was spent in a well-earned rest.

The transport arrived at the camp complete, and allowed of forage and rations being replenished. How it had been able to come through the enemy country by roads suitable for transport without being attacked, remained a mystery to those who do not know the circumstances! During the day thousands of Turkish and German prisoners were marched along the road from Beisan, usually in the charge of only a few mounted men.

CHAPTER 22

To Haifa and Acre

The next day (September 23rd), everything having been cleared up in this district, the Division set out for Haifa and Acre on the coast. A glance at the map will show that these towns are about 12 miles distant from each other, both being about 23 miles from Nazareth—there being two separate roads. The northern road to Acre was taken by the 13th Brigade and the southern to Haifa by the 15th and 14th. As regards our Squadron the first part of the journey to Haifa was just in the nature of a "route march," although the pace ridden was fast at times. The 15th Brigade was the leading one and the 13th Brigade as stated above made straight to Acre from Nazareth. Passing through El Fule the 15th and 14th followed the railway for some distance, then bearing off to the right they joined the main road from Nazareth to Haifa along the hills bordering the plain.

From Sheikh Abreik—the highest point on the road—the sea could be seen in the distance, a beautiful blue, whilst a refreshing breeze met the face. A short distance further on, a halt was made. During this the sound of guns was heard in the distance from the direction of the sea.

No opposition having been expected, all sorts of reports came down the column concerning the cause of the firing, such as (1) British destroyers in the bay have mistaken the 15th Brigade for the enemy and (2) The enemy have got a naval gun with which they are shelling the head of the column!

But all rumours proved to be false. What was really happening was the Turkish garrison at Haifa (about 1,000 strong) with field and machine-guns were defending the town against our advance—a hopeless affair, considering that they were entirely cut off, without any chance of obtaining supplies or reinforcements.

The Sherwood Rangers went to the assistance of the 15th Brigade which really had a very difficult task, as the plain before Haifa was, in many places, boggy and almost impassable; in addition there were many streams flowing across it. The main road to Haifa runs right along the foot of Mount Carmel on the left of the plain, and bordering it. It was here that the enemy had established themselves, covering every part of the ground with their guns. With great dash, however, the 15th Brigade galloped the enemy positions, and within a short time had captured the town! Much to everybody's regret, the son of General Sir Pertab Singh was killed during this attack. His loss was much regretted by his comrades, and all who knew him.

While this action was taking place, we (the 14th Brigade) descended the hill from Sheikh Abreik, crossed a bridge, which was at a great height over the river Kishon, and, turning to the right off the road, dismounted and watered from it with buckets. It was here that, owing to over-keenness on the part of two horses in the Squadron, they broke away, and, trying to drink from the river, fell in! Fortunately both were rescued, but not without great difficulty. Meanwhile, shelling was going on; luckily the shells all fell short of us, although having descended the hill, as mentioned, we had attracted the attention of the Turkish gunners. Later on in the day we moved into Haifa along the road which had been the scene of the action. Passing the results of the work of the 15th Brigade and of the "S.R.Y." which, to judge from the numbers of killed and wounded along the road (which were being dealt with by the Cavalry Field Ambulance), must have been of a very strenuous character, we at length encamped upon the sea-shore, under date palms, within a mile north of the town! The distance covered that day was 25 miles.

The 13th Brigade, meantime, had captured Acre on the north, after only slight opposition, yet it had effected, within a few hours, the feat which Napoleon had entirely failed to accomplish after a siege of 60 days! Incidentally, it may be mentioned, that heaps of his cannon-balls were found at Haifa.

The next morning (24th), our men and horses bathed in the sea! A short distance out, underwater, it was found that barbed wire had been fixed. This the Turks had evidently placed in position with the object of preventing a landing from the sea. These entanglements, however, in no way impeded the bathing as they could easily be seen in the clear water. Our troops were also allowed to visit the town, which was found to be very interesting; there being many modern houses, it was, in several respects, superior to any town we had previously visited in the interior. It is not too much to say that many of the inhabitants were delighted to see the British. They even said that they had expected us the previous year!

CHAPTER 23

Capture of Damascus

After another day spent at Haifa, back again the Division went (leaving the "S.R.Y." as a garrison), along the same road by which they had come, as far as the top of the hill above the river. Here we branched off to the left through Beit Lahm (a German colony), and Seffurie to Kefr Kenna, four miles north-east of Nazareth on the Tiberias Road, said to be the "Cana of Galilee" where the water was turned into wine. The latter part of the road was very narrow and rocky, being in parts merely a goat-track. Our animals had no water that day—it being quite unobtainable in spite of previous advices.

At 02.00 the next morning (September 26th) the Division started for Tiberias. "No. 1" Section going with the advance guard, the remainder of the Squadron following the Deccan Horse. The 14th Brigade reached the shores of Lake Tiberias (Sea of Galilee) just north of the town at 08.30 and halted until 12.00 to allow the Australian Mounted Division to pass through on their way towards Damascus. Here, horses were "off-saddled" and watered twice during the halt, the water being quite fresh and clear. Being upon the shore, which was gently shelving, they were able to walk in and drink to their hearts' content. A number of men also took the opportunity to bathe; it was fairly hot, being 680 feet below the level of the sea.

The River Jordan runs right through the lake, and it is interesting to know now that this point was 64 miles (as the crow flies), up the river from the site of the late Squadron camp when it was previously in the Jordan Valley. It was reported to us that the 4th Division had had tough work in the streets of Tiberias in order to capture it. They had now gone round the southern shores of the lake and joined forces with the Sherifian Troops, who had been harassing the enemy's Fourth Army east of the Jordan and were now pursuing them northwards. Practically the whole of the Turkish Seventh and Eighth Armies, which previously held the line west of the Jordan, had now been accounted for.

At 12.00 we continued the advance along the shores of the lake through pleasant, cultivated country, to the north-west corner; then northward, for about six miles, and down an avenue of trees, past the pretty little Jewish village of Jataine.

The Australians, in front, were held up at Kusa Atra on the Jordan by artillery and machine-guns at the bridge, which the enemy had destroyed. That night the 14th Brigade encamped within two miles of this bridge, having marched over 30 miles that day. Early the next morning (September 28th) the Australians crossed the river by the ford, and "scuppered" the party which had been holding them up, but, unfortunately, with the loss of a few of their number. The 14th Brigade accordingly moved down to the river at 09.00 and watered, and at 15.00 crossed by the bridge which had, by then, been repaired by the Royal Engineers ("No. 2" Section with advance guard fording), and continued north-easterly along what would have been a good road with the help of a steam roller (but at present was the reverse, owing to the large stones put down not being rolled in), to Kuneitra (14 miles by the map but actually hardly less than 20), arriving 23.00.

The next day we rested. Troops having been sniped at by natives, a party from the Squadron was detailed to make an example of two offenders who had been caught "red-handed". They were taken back to their village, and after their crime had been publicly announced by an interpreter to the chief of the tribe and the inhabitants, they were shot by the firing party. At 18.00 the Brigade moved off through the village along the main Damascus Road. About nine miles out they were brought to a halt, as the Australians in front were "held up". Later, they cleared the way, however, and we moved on again at 04.30. A halt of half an hour was made at 07.00 to water in the Nahr Mughaniye, after which part of the distance was covered at the trot. At 11.30 the head of the column reached Khan-esh-Shiha, 14 miles south-east of Damascus.

The enemy was seen on the Deraa Road, eight miles to the east, retreating northward, evidently being chased by the 4th Division and Hedjaz troops (Sherifians). It was reported by aeroplanes that the enemy force numbered about 3,000, and the 14th Brigade (less the one regiment left at Haifa), was allotted the task of cutting them off.

Turning to the right across country, we proceeded at a fast pace through fields of maize, gardens, orchards and then open country, arriving at the hills north of Kiswe over-looking the Deraa Road. These we occupied, and came in touch with the enemy who had sent out troops to attack. "No. 1" Section was in action along with two squadrons of Deccan Horse. They only reached their positions a few minutes in front of the enemy's flank guard, who, owing to the steepness and rocky nature of the ground, was able to approach within a few yards of the guns before being re-pulsed. During this encounter it is much regretted that Pte. Staniland was killed.

"No. 2" Section was in action on the hill occupied by Brigade Headquarters against the enemy, on a hill 600 yards to the front. After repulsing them, they went round and occupied the hill, being joined shortly afterwards by "No. 1" Section. Here an extensive view was obtained of the surrounding country—in front, the Deraa Road from Kiswe village and station, on the right (and beyond) and on the left the town of Damascus itself. It is impossible to imagine a more beautiful sight than that which Damascus presented from this spot, with its white minarets shining in the sunlight, above the orange groves, vineyards and orchards which surround it. The panorama was more particularly striking because of the contrast it presented with the rest of the country we had previously seen. Some good "shooting" was obtained from here, and the road was soon cleared. Parties of the enemy could be seen making off eastward up the hills, but out of range. The railway from Damascus runs parallel to the road, and beyond it. A train which was then en route was fired at, but it was also rather out of range.

Just then the Turk got some field guns in action and sent a few shells over at us, the very first one falling right on top of Brigade Headquarters; fortunately, it did not hit anyone!

"No. 3" Section accompanied the Poona Horse on the left flank, and there had some "practice" on the road, similar to the other sections. It was joined there by "D" Sub-section, Nos. 1 and 2 having come out of action, as there were no further "targets" for them. "No. 1" Section was now sent, with one squadron of Deccan Horse, to occupy a hill south-east of Ashrafie and due north of the position they had been holding. Machine-gun fire was met with half a mile from the hill, but only one casualty was sustained (Pte. Knott, wounded). The Deccan Horse charged the hill, and the section came in action on the top of it, firing upon the retreating enemy and silencing two of their machine-guns. The groves round Ashrafie, and the road to the east, were "traversed" and a regiment of Turkish cavalry, which was in the groves, at length sent a representative under a white flag expressing a desire to surrender. Outposts were now put out, and the remainder of the Brigade was moved up to Ashrafie and watered, staying in that vicinity for the night.

Some splendid grapes and other minor luxuries were obtained at the village and were very acceptable. That night the country was lit up for miles around, and the air resounded with explosion after explosion by the destruction of large ammunition dumps and other stores by the Turks. "No. 3" Section remained with the outposts, owing to the fact that two orderlies who had been sent out were unable to find them.

In the early morning they obtained some splendid "targets" on the road, against the tail of the Turkish force which was being driven along by the 4th Division and the Hedjaz troops. Close on their heels came Lieut.-Col. Lawrence and Major Sinclair of the Sherifian Army in a car. They would have been fired on, but for the fact that our own troops were in the danger zone. Their identity was discovered in time, however, and Major Davies, who had just arrived to see how "No. 3" Section was faring, went down and spoke to them.

At 07.30 the Australians having got round to the north of the city, our Brigade moved through Ashrafie and groves eastward to the road, so frequently referred to above, and marching along it, passed Meidan, at 09.30 entering Damascus—just 12 days from the start of operations, it being then October 1st 1918. The approximate distance covered by the Division was 215 miles, the distance due north of our old Line 104 miles.

Probably the town of Damascus proved to be disap-

115

pointing to the majority of the troops. It was interesting, certainly, but those who had been long in the East did not find the expression "Eastern splendour" realised here, any more than in other towns they had seen; such an idea would seem to exist only in the minds of those who have never been "out East". The natives, on the whole, seemed pleased to see us, the victors, and frequently cheered, while Major L.F. St. J. Davies, M.C., at the head of the Squadron (which followed the Poona Horse, the leading regiment, thus being the first white troops), was exceedingly popular.

In accordance with the Arab custom, when rejoicing, rifles were fired in the air—and this not with "blank" either!

Right through the centre of the town, the Brigade went, and camped in olive groves along the main road, leading out to the north-east. The following day it retraced its steps to the south of the town where it joined the "C.-in-C.". He had with him the remainder of the Division and the Australians. A triumphal entry into the town with the troops named was then made.

The Machine-Gun Squadron, given the choice, went independently, straight to their next camp at El Judeide, nine miles south-west of Damascus, preferring to rest their horses. There they camped in orange groves, being re-joined in the evening by the remainder of the Brigade, who had taken part in the "show".

Sec.-Lieut. Arden in the meantime was having an adventure "on his own". When we were ordered back to El Judeide Mr. Arden was told to go into the town and make all the purchases he could, so as to provide the Squadron with a few comforts. He took with him Q.M.S. Fisher, the officers' mess cook, and his groom. Having made his purchases, Mr. Arden, who had been told that our destination was on the western road, looked it up on the map and found a place marked there on the road to Beyrout about 10 miles distant named "El Jedeide". Off they started for this El Jedeide. What an experience they had! The road, which had just previously had the close attention of the R.A.F. and other branches of the service, was littered with dead and all kinds of enemy material. Along they continued, meeting everywhere sights of wreck and confusion such as they had never previously experienced. Having reached Jedeide, but failing to find any trace of British troops, they felt they had made a mistake. But it was too late to return that night, and there was no help for it, they were forced to spend the night there "and trust to luck".

Alternately taking post "on guard," some sleep was obtained. During the night some troops passed by, which the small party feared was Turkish; fortunately they turned out to be French Colonial Troops, whose dress is somewhat in the Turkish fashion. At daylight the party retraced its steps toward Damascus, and on the way, met a party of Australians. "What the devil are you doing here?" the latter demanded. Upon hearing their story the Australians ejaculated: "Why, do you know you have been for one night the outpost of the British Army? No British soldier has been here before"! But "all's well that ends well"; in due course, after minor adventures, Mr. Arden's party reached the Squadron at El Judeide where, although he had to run the gamut of chaff and banter, he was heartily welcomed!

CHAPTER 24

The Valley of Lebanon-Rayak

Henceforward, the 5th Cavalry Division was to become an entirely separate force in its operations—indeed, at one time, its nearest support was 100 miles distant. Two days were spent at El Judeide, grazing horses and cleaning guns and saddlery, before making another move forward. A force of Turks some 7,000 strong was reported to be at Rayak Junction on the Beirut Railway 30 miles north-east of Damascus, and on October 5th at 06.00 the Division, with the 14th Brigade leading (the "S.R.Y." had re-joined from Haifa), set off to deal with them. "No. 2" Section was with the advance guard.

Across country to Sabura, they reached the main Beirut Road at Khan Dimez, 15 miles from Damascus, and halted for the night at Khan Meizebun a few miles further on, with outposts out. Following the road to the bridge over the river, south of Bar Elias (where a halt for water was made), the advance guard ("No. 1" Section with it), was much surprised at the extraordinary behaviour of the natives, who, sighting them from a distance, galloped to meet them, firing their rifles in the air and shouting. Such was their method of giving us welcome; it would have been their own fault if they had been mistaken for the enemy, as they very nearly were!

At this point, turning north along a track up the Valley of Lebanon (many miles wide) the Brigade pushed on to Rayak. All along the road, right from Khan Dimez, the previous day, there was evidence of the sorry plight of the Turk. Hundreds of dead horses, dead bodies (stripped by the villagers), broken wagons and even overturned "gharries" strewed the route.

Upon our approaching Rayak, as if at a word of command, suddenly, a tremendous burst of rifle fire broke out! This outburst, however, proved to be merely a demonstration of the population's welcome! Rayak, and some of the villages in this district, are Christian, and it may well be imagined that the population was simply delirious with joy at the arrival of the British.

As the Brigade marched through the streets on each side there were crowds of people occupied in competing with each other to keep up the most rapid fire! They were none too particular where their shots went either!! It was rather difficult for us to feel pleased to see our new friends, when they were letting off their rifles under our very noses! Fortunately there were no casualties from the spent bullets, but there were several very narrow escapes! The Turk, it seemed, had fled two days previously, and left at the aerodrome the remains of no fewer than 30 aeroplanes which he had burnt, together with large quantities of stores and rolling stock.

An outpost line was established at Hosh el Ghanin, and "No. 1" Section returned to the Squadron, which had encamped to the east of the town south of the village of Maazi. October 7th-12th were spent in grazing, cleaning up and resting (not much of the last). On Oct. 10th, the 13th and 14th Brigades had moved on four miles to Tel esh Sherif, the 15th Brigade being at Zahle, a fair-sized town on the slopes of the hills on the western side of the plain.

At this time enemy aeroplanes began to arrive, and drop bombs, killing, on one occasion, some Gloucesters. A few days afterwards they were chased to their lair by the R.A.F. and—finished off!

The 14th Brigade, following the 13th Brigade one day's march behind, moved up to Baalbek on October 13th. Here we ascertained that the leading brigade had had a similar reception to ours from the natives at Rayak. Passing through the town and the ruins of the celebrated Roman Temple of the Sun on the left, we camped east of the Turkish barracks.

North of Baalbek our maps were found to be very inaccurate and unreliable, the actual position of places often proving to be many miles away from where shown; frequently roads followed quite a different route! In one place a railway line was omitted altogether from the map, while in another, a river marked thereon did not exist!

Rations, now being brought up by motor lorries nearly every day, were issued to units as soon as they had camped for the night; mutton was the principal meat ration, sheep being requisitioned locally, all along the route, as also was forage.

The transport was now able to follow close behind the Brigade, and usually arrived in "camp" shortly after the fighting troops. The "trek" now became a matter of routine, marching usually starting each day at 07.00. Permission was given for the Squadron to carry some of its guns on its transport, in order to relieve the pack-animals.

October 14th—To Lebwe; watering from a stream on the way, and camping in groves.

October 15th—To El Kaa. The Squadron camped against a fig-grove and figs were purchased for everyone.

October 16th—To Kusseir. Camp on plain east of station.

October 17th—To Homs. When about half way, in front

could be seen what appeared to be a large camp of bell tents, but on getting nearer they turned out to be merely a village of mud huts of that shape, and whitewashed!

Afterwards many similar villages were met with, some of which were whitewashed, some not. From hereabouts could be seen, away on the left, the large Homs Lake, through which runs the River Orontes (Nahr el Asi). Two miles south of the town of Homs an hour's halt was made to allow of watering and feeding, then passing a ruined castle on an artificial mound, we went through the centre of the town (which is an interesting old place, and apparently well supplied with water), to the main road out to the north. Then, along a track to the north-west, we passed the 13th Brigade camp (the 13th Brigade had been a day ahead from Tel esh Sherif) and bivouacked at 14.45 on a nice piece of ground on the banks of the Orontes, against the village of Deir Mati.

CHAPTER 25

The March to Aleppo

Would we stay here at Homs, or go still further? was the question uppermost in the minds of all. The nearest troops were at Damascus 100 miles behind us, and Aleppo, the next town of any importance, 100 miles ahead. We had now covered 325 miles in 28 days, and a rest was much needed. The question was soon decided for us! Three days were occupied in washing (men, clothes and horses), grazing and cleaning saddlery. Then, at 07.00 on October 21st we set out on our long journey, the 15th Brigade (it being their turn to lead), having left the day previously. Marching was carried on in accordance with the following: twenty minutes' trot, one hour's walk, 10 minutes' halt; and the following were the day's marches:

October 21st—To Er Rastan.

October 22nd.—To Hama. Through the town and over the River Orontes past the huge water wheels for which it is famous. These wheels make a loud humming noise and can be heard for miles. They are used for lifting the water from the river, which is between high cliffs at this point, to irrigate the surrounding country.

October 23rd.—To Khan Shaikhun.

October 24th.—To Ma'arit en Na'aman, camping east of the town. In the afternoon rain came on and continued overnight. It was the first rain of the season.

October 25th.—To Seraikin, camping against some groves south-east of town.

October 26th.—At 05.00 to Khan Tuman. The ground being suitable, the 14th Brigade marched with its Squadrons in line of troop column on the right of the road, and the 13th Brigade in the same formation on the left, while the transport was in the centre, on the road itself.

Early in the afternoon, arriving at the banks of the Kuwaik-Su, the stream that flows through Aleppo from the north, the 20th Machine-Gun Squadron off-saddled and settled down, the latest information being that they would not be required till morning. However, orders were shortly received to continue the advance to Aleppo! The guns were also to be withdrawn from the transport. The Squadron therefore moved off with the Brigade about 17.00.

What had been happening in front, in the meantime? No definite news was to hand, but an armoured-car tender came back for a fresh supply of "S.A." ammunition for the 15th Brigade Machine-Gun Squadron, so evidently some fighting had taken place. We had already heard that armoured cars, which had for some time past been doing "yeoman service," had arrived before Aleppo and scattered enemy patrols, and that an officer had been to the town and demanded its surrender. He was received with every courtesy, but the gallant commander regretted that he was unable to surrender the city as he had received orders from Constantinople to hold out at all costs, in order to cover the retirement of the Mesopotamian forces! That was some days previously. Later, we learnt that on the day in question, the 15th Brigade, having arrived before the "city gates," the Turks withdrew after destroying bridges, etc., and they (the Brigade) pushing on, met them on the Alexandretta Road, put spurs to their horses, and charged them.

Now, it may be remarked, the Turk outnumbered the 15th Brigade by at least five to one, and after the Brigade had passed through them, the enemy realised their strength, and picking up the very rifles they had thrown down, fired at their backs, Lieut.-Col. Holden and many other valuable lives being lost in this manner!

But the Turk had really no fight left in him; his was a beaten army! He continued his retreat, and the 15th Brigade took up an outpost-line north and north-west of the city.

The 14th Brigade heard of the capture of Aleppo when they arrived within a few miles of it after dark.

Reaching the southern outskirts of the town, they entered it by the road leading past the prison up to the Clock Tower. Leaving this on the right, they turned sharply to the left (past the present Officers' Club) almost up to Divisional Headquarters (then already established), where they bore to the right, down to the bridge under the railway, at the French railway station. The bridge had been blown up and a truck which was hanging down, completely blocked the roadway, causing considerable delay, as the whole Brigade had to lead their horses in "single file" up the steep embankment, across the railway lines, and down the other side, in order to regain the road. Two and a half miles along the Alexandretta Road the Brigade turned to the left off the road, east of Bileramum, and halted for the night, it being then 23.45.

The next morning, at 05.30, the 14th Brigade took over the outpost-line from the 15th Brigade. The Deccan Horse and "No. 3" Section held the ground west of the road. The Poona Horse and "No. 1" Section held the road itself and east of it. An enemy rearguard patrol was seen retiring, and was followed up by Sherifian troops, but nothing more was seen of the Turk. During the morning the 13th Brigade took over the ground to the west of the road, thus relieving the Deccan Horse and "No. 3" Section. "No. 2" Section relieved "No. 1" Section.

At night, "No. 1" Section with "S.R.Y." and "No. 3" with Deccan Horse took over the line. Members of the Squadron who took part in the operations from Khan Tuman onwards, will remember that "No. 2" and "No. 3" Sections, owing to shortage of personnel due to sickness (principally malaria or dysentery), had only been able to man three guns each, instead of their full complement of four, so that when "No. 2" Section was on duty "No. 3" Section supplied a detachment to make them complete, "No. 2" doing the same when "No. 3" was on duty, whilst in order to have all the guns in the Squadron available in case of emergency, the Squadron headquarter troops manned the remaining two guns. The next two days (October 28th and 29th) the outpost-line was still held, and nothing in the way of active operations occurred; men not on duty were granted passes to visit Aleppo.

CHAPTER 26
Armistice With Turkey

On the morning of October 30th, our Brigade was relieved by the "13th," and moved eastwards across the railway, then northward to Muslimie Junction. No enemy being encountered, an outpost line was established about two miles north, "No. 1" Section with "S.R.Y." and "No. 2" (with one detachment of "No. 3") with the Poona Horse. The latter section was entirely alone during the day, as it was not considered necessary to have so many troops on duty as at night time, and the Squadron being too far away to allow of the Section doing the double journey with any degree of comfort, it remained where it was.

At 12.00 on October 31st an armistice with Turkey was proclaimed, the good news being communicated to the Sections on outpost duty by orderlies from Headquarters. The Sections, however, had orders to remain at their posts. November 4th brought the further news of an armistice with Austria, and early the following day Indian prisoners, released by the Turks, began to return to us through our outpost line.

It was at this time that Major Davies, our O.C. (who had not been well since leaving the Jordan Valley, and for some time past had only been able to keep out of hospital by dint

MUSLIMIE JUNCTION STATION

of great strength of mind and powers of endurance, in spite of the advice of his own, and medical, officers), was at last sent to the hospital in Aleppo, which had been established by the 14th C.F.A. He had only been there a few days, however, when, to the grief of all, he passed away in the clutches of that dread disease, malignant malaria.

He was buried in the Aleppo Protestant Cemetery on November 11th 1918, in the presence of the Divisional Commander, the Brigade Commander, the C.O.'s of all the units in the Brigades, and many members of his Squadron, all of whom felt how regrettable it was that he had not been spared to hear *the great news* which we all then felt was so close at hand, and towards the obtaining of which he had, ever since the outbreak of the War, contributed so much energy and ability. The "H.A.C." kindly provided us with a gun-carriage upon which to convey him to his resting place, and Capt. Powell, C.F., the Brigade Chaplain, officiated.

As those who had been present at the ceremony were waiting for the motor lorries to take them back to Muslimie the momentous news was received that an armistice had been signed with Germany!

It was universally felt to be a sad coincidence that he who had come through the war from start to finish should thus have been laid low at the very end of his labours. That Major St. John Davies, M.C., was undoubtedly a great leader and very considerate of his men's welfare, was universally known. There can be no doubt that he would have had a successful career, had he been spared, in any profession he might have chosen.

Malaria was taking its toll, and a few days later Signaller Boak, who had been the Squadron's Brigade Orderly throughout the last operations, fell another victim to its clutches. He was buried in the Military Cemetery, Aleppo, a number of his comrades being present at the graveside.

Capt. R.H. Fairbairns, M.C., now took command,

with Lieut. A.O.W. Kindell as Second-in-Command. The strength of the Squadron was now four officers, 145 O.R.'s, 116 riding horses, 77 draught mules, 36 pack animals, and, as no reinforcements had reached the Squadron since the start of operations on September 19th, these figures represented a loss of two officers, 67 O.R.'s, 65 riding horses, three draught mules and seven pack animals. Considering that the Squadron had covered 450 miles in 43 days, in addition to the fighting, the loss in animals (especially draught) was extremely small, and results show that the Squadron has every reason to be proud of its horsemastership.

The Sections were now withdrawn from "outpost" and the Squadron moved into Muslimie station, where a certain number of buildings appeared to be available, and capable of affording protection from the wet weather, which showed signs of coming on.

Unfortunately, after clearing out several buildings, these had to be relinquished to a regiment of the 15th Brigade, which came up to take over the station. The Squadron, however, was allowed to use, as billets, some old railway trucks which could not be moved, owing to the points being blown up. It was expected, at one time, that the Division would proceed to Alexandretta, on the coast, for the winter, but this did not eventuate.

About this time we had to say farewell to our old friend, Capt. Powell, C.F., the Brigade Padre, who was compelled to go into hospital after repeated attacks of malaria, and was eventually invalided home to England. Capt. Powell had been with the Brigade since its original formation as the "7th Mounted," and was a great favourite amongst all ranks.

The following brief record of the events and doings of the Squadron during its long spell of duty at Aleppo (and Muslimie) may be interesting to some readers:

1918

Nov. 13	"No. 3" Section absorbed in "Nos. 1 and 2".
Nov. 15	Inspection of horses by Corps Commander.
Nov. 17	Memorial service in main station building.
Nov. 18	Headquarters attached to "Nos. 1 and 2" Sections.
Nov. 22	Inspection of Transport by Divisional Commander.
Nov. 28	Inspection of horses by G.O.C. Brigade.
Nov. 30	Ration strength: 4 officers, 122 O.R.s, 208 animals.
Dec. 4	Divisional Commander inspects horses.
Dec. 5	Preparation for visit of "C.-in-C.".
Dec. 9	Capt. J.B. Oakley and Lieut. E.P. Cazalet, with 60 reinforcements, arrive from base. Capt. Oakley becomes Second-in-Command of Squadron.
Dec. 10	Four officers and 80 O.R.'s proceed to Aleppo mounted for
Dec. 11	"C.-in-C.'s" procession, and return to camp.
Dec. 17	Thanksgiving Day.
Dec. 24	"B" Echelon (and donkeys) arrive.
Dec. 25	Anthrax in Brigade.
Dec. 27	One case of anthrax in Squadron.

1919

Jan. 3	Inspection of Transport by Divisional Commander.
Jan. 4	"No. 1" Sub-section proceeds to Aleppo with two troops "S.R.Y." to escort "C.-in-C." by train to Jerablus.
Jan. 6	Return of party.
Jan. 20	Short range practice.
Jan. 25	Classes opened in Brigade for shorthand, engineering, lectures, etc.
Jan. 27	Coalminers leave for "demob.".
Jan. 28	G.O.C. Brigade inspects horses.
Feb. 1	Classification of horses: A.30, B.33, C.II.42, D.8.
Feb. 3	Divisional Commander inspects animals and first line transport.
Feb. 11	Orders to move to Aleppo. Dismounted party with surplus equipment proceeds by train.

Feb. 12	Squadron moves to Aleppo.
Feb. 14	Corps Commander visits lines during stables.
Feb. 19	Sec.-Lieut. Arden appointed Brigade Educational Officer and promoted Captain whilst so employed.
Feb. 20	Move to old 19th Squadron camp.
Feb. 23	Twenty-two farmers proceed "homeward" ("de mob." camp at Kantara).
Feb. 26	Div. Commander visits lines during stables.
Feb. 27	Eleven O.R.'s to "Homeward".
Feb. 28	An Armenian massacre; Squadron proceeds to centre of town, four guns in position, one sub-section ("D") to Brigade Headquarters for night.
Mar. 1-3	Fifteen O.R.'s "demob.".
Mar. 6	Move to camp in the centre of Aleppo.
Mar. 11	Twenty-seven horses evacuated to M.V.S.
Mar. 17	Farewell parade to the G.O.C., Desert Mounted Corps, Lieut.-Gen. Sir H.G. Chauvel, K.C.B., K.C.M.G.
Mar. 19	Fifteen reinforcements arrive from base.
Mar. 20	Twenty horses and 26 mules to Corrals (paddocks formed by the Division to take the surplus animals resulting from demobilization).
Mar. 27	One sub-section short-range practice.
Mar. 29	Eleven horses and 32 mules to Corrals.
Mar. 31	Squadron strength: four officers, 124 O.R.'s, 185 animals.
Apr. 1	G.O.C. Brigade inspects horses.
Apr. 3	One sub-section short-range practice.
Apr. 15	"Stand-to" 05.30-08.00, one sub-section mounted, six guns on limbers.
Apr. 16	Ditto (as precaution against further massacre of the Armenians).
Apr. 22	Practice scheme with Brigade.
Apr. 23	Issue of summer clothing.
Apr. 30	Divisional Horse Show.
May 1-2	Ditto. Squadron won Special Prize with pack mule "Pansy," and had one limber and G.S. wagon in final; Pte. Carruthers also qualified for jumping finals.
May 31	Squadron strength: four officers, 75 O.R.'s, 189 horses and mules.

June 18	Inspection of horses and transport by Divisional Commander.
June 30	Peace celebrations. The Squadron, reduced to the strength of one sub-section, took part in "march past". Strength: three officers, 48 O.R.'s, 30 horses, 23 mules.

The following, by a member of the Squadron, is typical of the life in the *armies of occupation*. He says:—

Although these (the Armies of Occupation) officially have only existed since February 1st 1919, they have in reality, on certain fronts, been in operation since November 1918. The 5th Cavalry Division, pressing hard on the heels of the flying Turk, entered Aleppo on the evening of 26th October last. Trek-tired and weary, the Fighting Division under Major-Gen. H.J.M. MacAndrew, C.B., D.S.O., wound its lengthy column over the Kuwaik-Su Bridge and entered the ancient Turkish stronghold. Some of the units were at once stationed close to the town, taking over the barracks and vast stores and depots vacated by the enemy, whilst some of us, not so lucky, were pushed forward to Muslimie, the important junction of the Mesopotamian and Palestine Railways; and there formed a line of outpost defence, just 300 miles due north of the line held six weeks previously.

On the 4th November the Armistice with Turkey was signed, and shortly after several cavalry units were sent still further north to Killis, Jerablus (on the Euphrates), and Aintab, and the outpost line near Aleppo was thus no longer required. Now followed a period even more difficult to put up with than actual war itself. A trek of over 400 miles in a space of two months, following that nightmare of a sojourn in the Jordan Valley, had reduced the vitality of both man and horse to a very low ebb, and consequently the sick roll in both cases was large. Malignant malaria contracted in the valley took toll of many brave lives, and an outbreak of anthrax, coupled with debility, caused havoc among the horses.

Railway communication not being completed, and

roads rendered unfit by heavy rains, delayed the passage of canteen stores, and the rations had perforce to consist chiefly of mutton caught, killed and eaten the same day. Shall we ever forget the taste of it? Of course, we did get goat sometimes as a variation. Xmas Day was on the horizon and no hope of any puddings, but most units were able to produce some kind of Xmas dinner, and a pudding concocted from local ingredients. Followed special trains to the 'Palmtrees' Concert Party in Aleppo, and a fox hunt on New Year's Day. Whist drives and 'sing-songs' helped to break the deadly monotony of the long winter evenings, and during the day there was plenty to occupy one; roads to make in the mud, stones to be carted, buildings and shelters erected, and more than all, the attempt to get a little of the dirt off one's animal, and a little more flesh on his bones. After the 130 degrees or so of heat (in the shade) in the Jordan Valley, the cold in Syria, during the winter, seemed intense, and ice had frequently to be broken before the morning wash. The snow on the Taurus Mountains was not reassuring either, and firewood and coal became almost unobtainable.

The only beverages obtainable at this time were native wines and army rum, and as the former consisted chiefly of sweet Alicante, methylated cognac and Arak, one became quite a connoisseur of the latter and the different methods of making rum punch.

One Quartermaster-Sergeant in particular made quite a reputation for himself as a punch mixer, and I know that among his favourite ingredients were oranges, lemons, figs, condensed milk, cloves, nutmeg, pepper, ginger, boiling water.

New Year's Eve saw (and heard) an officers' dinner, and all those from far and near flocked to a small building near the station, and under the able Presidency of popular Lieut.-Col. Wigan, of the Sherwood Rangers Yeomanry, and the direction of a Yorkshire vet. and a Captain of the Deccan Horse, the Old Year (and in some cases two Old Years) was seen out amid a score of toasts, the fumes of aromatic punch, and the strain of a buckshee piano. Personally, I crossed eight sets of Bagdad railway track in three strides.

"THE BRIGADE RACE MEETING

In February the 14th Cavalry Brigade held a Race Meeting on a short grass track of two and a half furlongs, discovered hiding among the rocks. A 'totalisator' run by an Australian in the interest of the Brigade, was run on sound lines, and if your horse won you got your money back and a little over, which isn't the case with some totalisators that we know of! Several 'scurries' and mule races took place, and everyone enjoyed the fun thoroughly, especially the mules. The machine-gun element sprung a surprise on all by winning the Grand Prix, open to the 5th Cavalry Division, with 'Nobbler,' a horse which was to have run at Gaza in 1918, but was 'scratched' owing to lameness. 'Lion,' a mobilisation horse of the Sherwood Rangers, and a prime favourite, came in second, and both horses were ridden at 11-7.

"THE FIRST ALEPPO MEETING

In March the 14th Cavalry Brigade took over its Aleppo quarters from the 13th and the latter were moved many miles to the north, where they also held a local meeting. Capt. Fraser of the R.H.A. was now given the task of turning a waste piece of ground on the western side of the town into a racecourse, and, by dint of much hard work and begging of materials, he completed a quite good course of four furlongs. The Royal Engineers erected a grand stand of sandbags, and a totalisator. The first Aleppo Race Meeting was held on March 8th, and a goodly representative gathering of the army and civilian inhabitants of Aleppo assembled. After this, race meetings were held regularly every alternate Saturday throughout the summer. The course was laid on fairly level ground, and at the start of the season had a thin covering of grass, which, unfortunately, soon was burnt up by the fierce sun and worn bare by frequent use, being replaced afterwards by litter. Though at first only a four furlong 'scurry,' the course has now been extended to eight furlongs, and laid much in the same fashion as Kempton Park with a 'straight' of four furlongs and the remainder an oval. One drawback to this course is that it crosses a high road in two places. On race days mounted military police are stationed outside the rails to keep order, and British troops are on duty in the enclosures keeping the gates, serving refreshments, and assisting in the totalisator. The latest attraction has been the admirable rendering of popular music by the Band of the Queen's Bays.

"Incidents at the Races

Of amateur jockeys and gentlemen riders there have been plenty; among the most successful being Lieut.-Col. Vincent, R.A.S.C., Major Walker, R.A., Capt. Sir Robin Paul, Lieut. Dowling. We much missed Lieut. Stanley Wooten, of the Sherwood Rangers Yeomanry, who has hitherto been such a popular rider in the E.E.F. Major-Gen. Sir Harry MacAndrew, C.B., D.S.O., Lieut.-Gen. Sir H.G. Chauvel, K.C.B., K.C.M.G., have all, in turn, shown much interest in the races, and Gen. Geaffar Pasha, the Military Governor of Aleppo, and successor to Gen. Shukri Pasha (generally known to us as 'Sugary Parsnips'), often enters one of his beautiful Arab chargers in the Arab class races, and is often successful. His jockey rides in the colours of the Hedjaz Army, red, white, black and green.

But the horses are now paraded in the paddock, and we must go and inspect them. This is an Arab race, and all sorts of conditions of men and horses are in the ring, and a terrific hubbub is going on. Some of the ponies are well groomed, and fit, others thin and badly cared for. Some have long unkempt manes and tails, others are bedecked with beads and shells and long scarlet tassels. Saddle cloths of brilliant hue are numerous, while the riders are a curious and a motley assembly. Some barefoot, some booted and spurred (and a spur is a spur with

ALEPPO: SQUADRON CAMP IN THE TOWN

an Arab, something after the implement mother marks the pastry with). Others are in long flowing robes with the burnous and kafeia of the Bedouin flying in the wind, some with knives, some with swords, some with pistols, and some with sticks, and lastly two are dressed like real jockeys, and they know it, and show it too! Just now there is a little of chaos as half the competitors are evidently of the opinion that they should go round the paddock in one direction, while the other half wishes to go the reverse. Wherefore there is loud shouting and much gesticulating, with many 'Waheds' and 'Achmeds' and 'Macknoons'.

But there, the bell goes, and the starters begin to file out of the gate as they struggle out of the seething mass. Away down the course to the starting point; and here the starter will no doubt have his work cut out. A variegated crowd is lining the rails on the opposite side of the track. Turbaned Abduls and Yussefs, boys and little girls, men and donkeys, fruit-sellers, arabiyehs, camels, all in brightest colours and a pandemonium of noise. Stray pi-dogs are continually being warned off the course, and venerable Arab Sheiks who don't understand, and start for a nice walk along the wide grass track. Yes, there is plenty for the smart military policemen to do, and their burnished swords and bright shoulder epaulets flash in the sun as they 'chivvy' the crowd out of danger. In the officers' enclosure there are many strange types. Abdul Achmed Yussef is there with a scimitar in one hand like the Sultan of Turkey, and a huge white umbrella in the other hand, and on his head he wears a red tarbush.

Iskanderianabedian is there with his fat wife, and two fat daughters, all the latter in black silk gowns and white silk stockings, and if the girls' ankles aren't as thick as my calves, call me a liar, but this is the Turkish style of beauty you know. The better bred the fatter is their standard, and very nice too. Arab troops and Arab gendarmerie in their quaint spiked head-gear; while hundreds of British staff officers (where they come from, or what they do I don't know), with tabs of all colours (and as one officer remarked to me only the other day, 'When the blue and green tabs appear it's time to capture another town'!) And a sprinkling of combatant officers, English sisters, French attachés, and American Red Cross workers, represent the western world.

Now we go and place our solitary 10 pt. on a promising pony ridden by one of the two 'real' jockeys. It is all we can spare, as the Field Cashier happens to be away (as usual). Suddenly a bugle blows, and we hear the usual cry 'They're off!' But they aren't; at least two are and there's no stopping those two. No, they mean to carry on now; neck and neck they go, and soon they are round the distant corner, and thundering past the four furlong point. On they come shouting for Allah and Mohammed, and standing high in their stirrups they wave their sticks madly in the air, yelling at each other with all the frenzy of the faithful followers of El Islam! A dead heat they reach the post and gallop wildly on, to end up somewhere on the banks of the Kuwaik Su!

Now, the bugle goes again, and the start has really begun this time, the field getting away something like a compact lump. But soon they string out, and we notice our two orthodox men well in rear. This time the race is even more exciting, and as the post is neared the yells of defiance, the flowing robes, the waving arms and the bump, bump, bump of the riders brings pictures to the mind of the fiery followers of Saladin, or an attack by the Arabs in the 'Tragedy of the Korosko'.

Well, it's over at last, and our 'choice' and the other smartly dressed jockey are miles behind. But that doesn't matter as I hear the winner is only paying out 5 pt. Oh! that 'Tote'! Six races are the usual number run; and then the sun sinks behind the Taurus Mountains, the shadows fall long and blue, and the high-up Citadel, flanked by mosques and minarets, becomes bathed in the orange light of the setting rays. As the last horse is led in, the crowd flows back towards the town, and then the arabiyehs crack their whips, the camels grunt, the staff start up their motor cars, and the combatant officers with light hearts and lighter pockets mount their chargers, and wend their way back to camp.

Such is an Aleppo Race Meeting, and so do we attempt to pass the monotony of an enforced exile in a barren and a dreamy land.

Very soon the rain will come, and then the mud, and then we shall look for the Christmas parcels, British books, local papers, and more than all—that long-promised holiday for the Army-of-Occupation-Volunteer!!

CHAPTER 27

Epilogue

The following extract from a letter from an officer at Aleppo to a former "O.C." of the Squadron (now demobilized) will perhaps serve as a fitting close to the record of the service of the 20th Machine-Gun Squadron.

Aleppo
4-10-19
Dear.....

Just a line to let you know how we are getting on. The 14th B'de has been abolished and several Units disbanded. The Cadre of the Sherwoods also, who are now in the 13th Brigade, is going home, but there are only a few of them to go to U.K. The 20th M.G.S. is to be disbanded, and the personnel to go to the 19th Squadron. We got orders yesterday to wind up the '20th' and send the personnel to the '19th' and I have to report to the 10th Cav. Bde. at Homs. What for I don't know yet. One consolation, all the men but five are now eligible for U.K.!! Well, well, it can't be helped, and perhaps it is as well we were broken up now as the men will perhaps be home by Xmas if the Strike is over.

Hope you are enjoying 'Civvy' life.

Yours, &c., ——.

The following are extracts from *The Times* of the 24th

July 1919 and the *Daily Mail* of 28th July 1919. They will not be read without sincere regret by all those members of the 20th "M.G.S." who had previously served in the 5th Cavalry Division.

Major-General Sir Henry John Milnes Macandrew, K.C.B., D.S.O., died from heart failure, resulting from burns, on the 16th inst. in Syria, where he was serving in command of the 5th (Indian) Cavalry Division.

A son of the late Sir Henry Macandrew, of Aisthorpe, Inverness, he was born on August 7th 1866, and joined the 2nd Batt. Cameron Highlanders in 1884, being transferred to the Lincoln Regiment two years later. Entering the Indian Army in 1888, he joined the 5th Cavalry, to which regiment he belonged until his promotion to major-general in 1917, and of which he was honorary colonel when he died.

He had extensive staff experience, being a graduate of the staff college and having spent about one-third of his service in the Indian Army on the staff. He went through the Tirah Campaign as brigade transport officer in 1897-98 (dispatches and frontier medal with two clasps), and he served through the South African War in various capacities, gaining the South African medal and four clasps, the King's medal and two clasps, and the D.S.O., and being twice mentioned in dispatches. He was brigade-major to the Inspector-General of Cavalry in India in 1903-5.

He served in France on the staff of the Indian Cavalry divisions from 1914 till 1917, when he was promoted major-general and received command of the 5th Cavalry Division. His services in France secured four mentions in dispatches and the K.C.B. He proceeded to Palestine with the Indian Cavalry Corps, and served under General Allenby in his successful advance from the Egyptian border to Aleppo. The division under his command was prominent in these operations, and the general was mentioned by Sir Edmund Allenby in dispatches for his excellent services.

General Macandrew was well known as a rider across country and on flat. He earned the reputation

of being one of the best and most dashing of our cavalry leaders in the war, and his untimely death is a severe loss to the Indian Army. He married, in 1892, the
youngest daughter of Mr. H.R. Cooper, J.P., of Ball-
indalloch, Stirlingshire, and leaves a young daughter.

From *The Times*, July 24th 1919.

Cairo, Friday.

Major-Gen. H.J. Macandrew, commander of the
Fifth Division, stationed at Aleppo, died a tragic death
last week. His tunic had been cleaned with petrol and
was hanging in a room to dry when the general, wearing
pyjamas, entered smoking a cigarette. The petrol vapours
exploded, burning General Macandrew so severely that
he died in hospital a week later.—Reuter.

It is possible that too much petrol was used or that the
heat of the sun vaporised the petrol and thus rendered it
so easily inflammable. An exactly similar accident is not
recorded in our own climate.

From *Daily Mail*, July 28th 1919.

FRENCH IN SYRIA BRITISH WITHDRAWN

Cairo, Dec. 10th 1919.

In accordance with arrangements with the Govern-
ment concerned a change has been made in the military administration of Syria (north of Arabian Desert,
including Palestine and Cilicia), the Valley of Adana, and
Tarsus (which since the Allied occupation have been
under the Commander-in-Chief of the Egyptian Expeditionary Force). The administration of Cilicia and
the area known as "occupied enemy territory (west),"
including Lebanon, Beirut, Tripoli, and Alexandretta,
has been handed over to General Gouraud, the French
High Commissioner.

The British military posts in the Marash, Aintab,
Urfa, and Jerablus areas, where the administration remains under the Turkish authorities, have also been relieved by the French.

The territory known as "occupied enemy territory

(east)" including Damascus, Homs, Hamah, and Aleppo, has been handed over to the Arab administration under the Emir Feisul (whom the Syrians welcome).

All the British troops have been withdrawn from Syria, and the military administration of Syria by the British Commander-in-Chief has ceased.

Reuter

Members of the
20th Machine-Gun Squadron

Note: A copy of this list has been sent by post to the address of every member for verification before going to Press.

Author, 1st June 1920

Officers

Major L.F. ST. JOHN DAVIES, M.C., Antringham Rectory, North Walsham, Norfolk (Died 10-11-18).

Major R.H. FAIRBAIRNS, M.C., 63 Alleyn Park, Dulwich, S.E.

Capt. E. DAVIES, c/o Messrs. Cox & Co., 16 Charing Cross, S.W.

Capt. D. MARSHALL, M.C., Margaret Place, Dollar, Fife.

Capt. J.B. OAKLEY, Grimston Hill, York.

Capt. F.A. SPENCER, M.C., c/o Messrs. Sir C.R. McGrigor, Bart., & Co. Panton St., S.W.

Lieut. E.P. CAZALET, Brunswick Rd., Sutton, Surrey.

Lieut. E.B. HIBBERT, "Babworth," Watson Ave., Mansfield, Notts.

Lieut. A.O.W. KINDELL, Rolle Cottage, Bourne End, Bucks.

Lieut. G.M. KING, York House, Headroomgate Rd., St. Annes-on-Sea, Lancs.

Lieut. C.D. MACMILLAN, Brackenhurst Hall, Southwell, Notts.

Lieut. A.G.P. MILLMAN, Liskeard, Cornwall.

Lieut. H.A. PRICE, M.C., "Homewood," Branksome Ave., Bournemouth (killed).

Lieut. R. RAYNOR, Jingewick Rectory, Bucks.

Lieut. F.R. WILGRESS, c/o The Bank of Montreal, Waterloo Place, London.

Second-Lieut. J.K.W. ARDEN, "Mayhills," nr. Petersfield, Hants.

Second-Lieut. J.W. CUMMER, 1221 13 Avenue, West Calgary Alta, Canada.

146

Squadron Sergeant Majors

FISHER, H., 65 Crosby Rd., West Bridgford, Notts.
FLEET, T., M.M., 32 Trinity St., Dorchester, Dorset.
JACKSON, J.B., M.M., "Denstone," Rocester, Staffs.
LARWOOD, E., D.C.M., Thorpe Farm, Shadwell, Thetford.
PHILLIPS, H., 21 Sutherland Rd., Bow, London, E.
SALTER, E.G., 16 Grays Rd., Henley-on-Thames, Oxon.

Squadron Quartermaster Sergeants.

CRISP, J., 14 Spencer Rd., Mitcham, Surrey.
FISHER, H., See under S.S.M.'s.
HARRISON, N.M., Pocklington, Yorks.

Staff Farrier Sergeant

ROBERTSON, T., 85 Bo'ness Rd., Grangemouth, Scotland.

Sergeants

ANDERSON, W. (Farrier), Steetley Farm, Whitwell, nr. Mansfield, Notts.
BUCKINGHAM, T., Lower Hayford, nr. Weedon, Northants.
COLLETT, J.H., High Rd., Vange, Essex.
CONUEL, T. (Transport), "Elmton," Chesterfield, Derby.
DUGUID, L.W.J., 42 Blenheim Gardens, Reading.
FELL, R.O. (Transport), 14 King's Avenue, Rhyl, N. Wales.
GAGE, L., Camden Stores, Lower Bristol Rd., Bath.
GRICE, T., M.M., 70 Olbury Rd., Smethwick, Staffs.
HAWKINS, E.W., M.M., 26 Springfield Rd., Gorleston-on-Sea, Suffolk.
HAZLEHURST, C.E., Low St., Carlton, nr. Worksop, Notts.
HOLT, F.F., 18 Sandhill St., Worksop, Notts.
KIRKE, C. (Orderly Room), 6 Curzon St., Derby.
KEETLEY, H., S. Megby, nr. Mansfield, Notts.
KNOWLES, G., "Tredethy," Bodmin, Cornwall.
LEWIS, R., "Craiglea," Penparke, Aberystwith, N. Wales.
MORDEN, W.H., 89 Ashburton Avenue, Addiscombe, nr. Croydon, Surrey
(died at Havre, 4th March 1919, en route for home).
O'NEILL, W., Barford Cottages, Churt, nr. Farnham, Surrey.
PARKER, W.R. (Farrier), Hermitage St., Crewkerne, Somerset.
PEADON, S., 103 Nottingham Rd., Long Eaton, Derby.
PEARSE, T., Kingham, Chipping Norton, Oxon.
POTTS, C., 9 Castle Hill Square, Worksop, Notts.
POUNTAIN, J., 79 Derby St., Derby.
RAMSAY, G. (Orderly Room), 94 Highfields, Coalville, nr. Leicester.

ROBERTS, C, 319 Ropery Rd., Gainsborough, Lincs.
ROUSE, F., Park Rd., Mansfield, Woodhouse, Notts.
SNEDDON, H., West Calder, Midlothian.
THOMPSON, S.C. (Transport), 11 Canterbury Rd., West Croydon, Surrey.
WRIGHT, W.J.P., 3 Beacon Hill Rd., Newark, Notts.

CORPORALS AND LANCE-CORPORALS

ADCOCK, H., 34 York Terrace, Gainsborough, Lincs.
BAGGS, F., Brook House, West Malling, Kent.
BARRATT, J.G., Ashby Rd., Loughboro', Linc.
BARTHORPE, F., 2 Ebenezer Place, Gainsboro', Lincs.
BITCHILY, H., 37 Park Terrace East, Hors ham, Sussex.
BILHAM J. (Signaller Corporal).
BINNINGTON, C. (Signaller Corporal), "Beaconsfield," Anlaby Rd., Hull.
BRADLEY, W., 46 Healey St., Nottingham.
CARR, F., Doncaster (killed at El Tahta).
CHINNERY, T.A. (Signaller Corporal), 7 Ashmead Rd., St. John's, Lewisham, S.E.
CLARK, G.H., Syston, Leicester.
FAIRLEY, J., 2 Brandfield St., Edinburgh.
FOSTER, G. (Signaller Corporal), Sgt. 3rd M.G. Sqdn., Risalpur, N.W.F.P., India.
FOX, P.W., Rollerton Mill Farm, R.S.O., Notts.
FRANKLIN, R.H., 13 Hyde Park Corner, Leeds.
FULLER, E.J., 2 Surrey St., Luton, Beds.
GALWAY, L., 54 Firgrove Rd., Freemantle, Southampton.
GAVAGAN, T., The Bazaar, Shrewton, Wilts.
GILL, H., 98 St. Anne's Well Rd., Nottingham.
GREEN, A., 16 Maria St., West Bromwich, Staffs.
GORING, A.C. (Signaller Corporal), 92 Coleridge St., Hove, Sussex.
HALEY, J., 3 Queen Victoria St., Wakefield, Yorks.
HOLMES, C. (S/Smith Corporal), 56 Mar Hill Rd., Carlton, Notts.
HUGHES, J., Queens Walk, Nottingham.
HUTCHINGS, F.G., "Maesgwyn," Ton Pentre, Glamorgan.
INESON, C., 20 Primrose Lane, off Burton Rd., Leeds.
IRELAND, C, "Bay Villa," Rosehill Rd., Ipswich.
JAMES, J., 76 Llangyfelach St., Swansea, S. Wales.
KIDD, S., 18 Aviary Mount, Armley, Leeds.
KINGS, E., 1 King Barton St., Gloucester.
KNIGHT, T.N., 29 Millicent Rd., West Bridgford, Notts.
LAWSON, A.P., 36 Castle Terrace, Nottingham.
LAYCOCK, F.J., 34 Highcroft Terrace, Brighton.
MARRIOTT, A., 65 Nottingham Rd., Stapleford, Notts, (killed).
MELLETT, C.W. (Saddler Corporal), 1 Park Terrace, Hillingdon Rd., Uxbridge, Middlesex.
MOVERLEY, S., 26 Wharncliffe St., Hull.

NEAL, G., 16 Nova Scotia St., Failsworth, Lancs.

PALMER, C.P., 26 Drake St., Gainsborough, Lincs.

PATTERSON, W., 72 High St., Dumfries, Scotland.

ROE, A.E., 184 St. Paul's Rd., Canonbury, London, N.

ROGERS, L.B., 122 Hillaries Rd., Gravelly Hill, Birmingham.

ROSE, J.B., 44 Ball St., Wells Rd., Nottingham.

SEDDON, H., 54 The Avenue, Leigh, Lancs.

SHARPE, H.E., 138 Sherrard Rd., Forest Gate, Essex.

SMALL, F., Earls Common, nr. Droitwich, Worcester.

SMITH, C.C., West St., Oundle, Northants.

STOKES, H., Sir John Barleycorn Hotel, Cadnam, Southampton.

UFF, G., 28 St. James St., Walthamstow, London.

WADDLOW, J. (S/Smith Corporal), Marylands, Dogsthorpe, Peterborough.

WAKE, T., 14 Roxburgh Place, Heaton, Newcastle-on-Tyne.

WALSHAW, L.J., 56 Canon St., Belgrave, Leicester.

WILLMORE, A.C., 2B Lakefield Villas, Westbury Avenue, Wood Green, N.

WOODHOUSE, H., 11 Queen St., Whittingtonoor, Chesterfield, Derby.

PRIVATES

ACE, E., 7 Carlos St., Port Talbot, S. Wales.

ADAMS, C.W., Chapel Ash, Wolverhampton, Staffs.

ADDISON, A., High St., Navenby, Lines.

ALLEN, L., 20 Liddington St., Basford, Notts.

AMOR, L.G., Road Common, Southwick, Tunbridge Wells, Kent.

APPLEY, T., Station Rd., Laughton Common, Yorks.

ARNELL, F., 35 Fernie Avenue, Melton Mowbray, Leicester.

ARNOLD, H.T., 29 High St., Old Basford, Notts.

ASHALL, R., 5 Bolton St , Park Rd., St. Helens, Lancs.

ASHE, A.E., 5 Barley Close, Chippenham, Wilts.

ATTWATER, L. (Signaller), 22 Dryburgh Rd., Putney, S.W.

AVERILL, R., Fox and Hounds Hotel, Brynmenyn, Bridgend, Glam.

BAKER, A., The Row, Eltham, Kent.

BAKER, C.E.

BALL, F., 1 Gladstone Terrace, Bunbury St., Nottingham.

BARTRAM, R., Froy Moor Farm. Briston, Melton Constable, Norfolk.

BEESTON, T., The Green, Middleton, Winkworth, Derby

BOAK, G., 3 St. Thomas' Place, Stockport, Cheshire (died at Aleppo).

BOHN, A.

BOYLING, F., 1 Claughton Villas, Priory Rd., Dudley.

BRADY, W., 7 Mill St., Kingston-on-Thames.

BRAMALL, T., "Broom Cottage," Carlton, Worksop, Notts.

BRANTON, F., 306 High St., Walton, Felixstowe.

BRETT, J., Highland Cottages, Clavering Newport, Essex.

BROWNE, R.A., "Rosemoyne," Warwick Rd., Sutton, Surrey.

BUTCHER, P.F., 34 Nursery Rd., Chelmsford, Essex.

CANE, E.W., "The Hollies," Swallowfield, nr. Reading.

CAPEL, B., "Woodbine Cottage," Dysart, Fife (died 17th Oct. 1918).

CARDER, W., Raynes Park, nr. Braintree, Essex.

CARRUTHERS, W., Keppoch, Kardros, Dumbarton Scotland.

CASH, J., 17 Ard Lane, Kiverton Park, nr. Sheffield.

CHANTRY, P., 5 St. James' St., Grantham (died of wounds).

CHARTERS, H.J., "Loch Lomond," Cheltenham Rd., Southend-on-Sea.

CHATTERTON (Transport), Flixton, nr. Manchester.

CHILDS, J.L. (S/Smith), "Holly Bank," Bourne End, Bucks.

CHIPPENDALE, E., 30 Moore St., Nelson, Lancs.

CLARKE, F.J., Post Office, Harpole, Northants.

CLARKE, H., 450 Leeming St., Mansfield, Notts.

CLARKE, S.H., 112 Aberdeen Rd., Winson Green, Birmingham.

CLARKE, W.E., Middle St., Wickham Market, Suffolk.

CLARKE, W.J., 88 Whitley Wood Lane, Reading, Berks.

CLAY, T., 24 High St., Kimberley, Notts.

CLAYTON, H., 3 Rutland Terrace, Meadows, Nottingham.

CLUTTEN, E.G., Church House, Wangford, Suffolk.

COLES, A.R. (S/Smith), The Forge, Epwell, Banbury.

COLLIER, A., 12 Rice St., New Basford, Notts.

COMRIE, G.E.L., 15 Dixon Avenue, Crosshill, Glasgow.

COOK, J., 32 Glen St., Paisley, Scotland.

COOKE, H.S., 19 Rosina St., High St., Homerton, N.E.

COOPER, J.E., Easton Royal Farm, Pewsey, Wilts.

CORY, P.F.P., Morecombe Farm, Milton Damerell, Brandis Corner, Devon.

COWELL, E., 47 Earl St., Lower Broughton, Manchester.

COX, A., 17 Belvedere St., Mansfield, Notts.

COZENS, C.F., 27 Acres St., Wandsworth, S.W.

CRANE, W.R., 6 Seventh Row, Ashington, Northb.

CRANFIELD, F., 72 Farnley Rd., South Norwood, S.E.

CROSSMAN, H., Bridgwater, Somerset.

CUNDALL, C.F., 12 Milton St., Middlesbrough, Yorks.

CURTIS, J., 96 Merchant St., Bullwell, Nott.

CURTIS, W., Royston House, Misterton, Doncaster, Yorks.

DALE, A.M., Crawford Gardens, North Down, Cliftonville, Margate.

DAVIES, C.L., 32 Carlton Rd., Sneinton Market, Notts.

DAVIES, H.C.P. (S/smith), 13 Artesian Rd., Bayswater, W.

DEWEY, C., 192 Ealing Rd., South Ealing, W.

DIPLOCK, P.H., 8 Everest Rd., Eltham, Kent.

DOWNS, A.F., Alnwick Villas, Gedling Rd., Carlton, Notts.

DRANSFIELD, D.V., Newlands Farm, Mansfield, Notts.

DRANSFIELD, S.A., Newlands Farm, Mansfield, Notts.

DREW, T.C., 25 Hamilton Rd., Long Eaton, Notts.

DROUET, A.G.E., "Ajow House," Speedwell Rd., Egbaston, Birmingham.

DUNCAN, J.C., 1 Wellgate, Kirriemuir, Forfar.

EALDON, E., 11 Railway Terrace, Sittingbourne, Kent.

EDGAR, W.J., 73 Sugarfield St., Belfast.

EDWARDS, A., 44 Greaves Rd., Lancaster.

EDWARDS, A.E., 18 Prospect Terrace, King's Cross, N.

ELLAMS, G., Capenhurst, nr. Chester.

ELLIOTT, G.W., 51 Shipstone St., New Basford, Notts.

ELLIS, C.L. (S/smith), 4 King Edward Rd., Brentwood, Essex.

ELPHICK, J., 15 George St., Fishergate, Sussex.

EWELS, P., Preston-on-Severn, nr. Shrewsbury.

FARDELL, A., 3 Hertford St., Colchester, Essex.

FARMER, J., 103 Newcombe Rd., Handsworth, Birmingham.

FEAR, J., 1 Greenhill Cottages, Cwmtillery, Wales.

FEWELL, H.P., 162 Upper Bridge Rd., Chelmsford, Essex.

FLETCHER, W., 54 Cranmer St., Nottingham.

FLORY, C., 7 Castle Rd., Colchester, Essex.

FOSTER, S., Wharncliffe Nurseries. Christchurch Rd., Boscombe.

FOX, W.H., 7 Nelson Terrace, Hutchinson St., Nottingham.

FRANCIS, H., Broxhall Farm, Lower Hardis, Canterbury.

FRANCIS, R.C., The Dairy, Woolaton, Notts.

FROST, E., c/o Mrs. Coleman, Forest View, Skegley, Notts.

FRYER, C.S., "A" Squadron, M.G.C. (Cav.) Depot Shorncliffe.

GALLAGHER, C. (Signaller), 47 Alderson Rd., Liverpool.

GARDNER, S.J.M., Billingford, Scole, Norfolk.

GENT, A., Baggholme Rd., Lincoln.

GILL, J., 117 Gloucester Rd., Bootle, Liverpool.

GODFREY, W., 1 Gladstone St., Carlton, Notts.

GOLDIE, H.C., 12 Morpeth St., Spring Bank, Hull (died of wounds, 3-12-1917).

GOODWIN, C.S., 24 Hawksley Rd., Nottingham.

GOODWIN, G., Robine Cossall, nr. Nottingham.

GRANT, R., 5 Gilburn Place, Bo'ness, Scotland.

GREENBAUM, ——, 94 Bridge St., Burdett Rd., London, E.

GREENBURY, W.H., 73 Sleaford, Newark, Notts.

GREGORY, R.H., "Pomona House," Furlong Avenue, Arnold, Notts.

GREIG, L.C., Braunstone, Leicester.

GRESSWELL, W.F., 110 Percival Rd., Sherwood, Notts.

GRIFFITHS, W., 43 East Side, Prendergast, Haverfordwest.

GYTE, J., Taylor Barn, Wessington, nr. Alfreton, Derby.

HADDEN, W.E., 228 Sharland Rd., Maida Hill, London.

HALL, J.E., 10 Clark St., Leicester.

HALLAM, F., 45 Labden St., Long Eaton, Derby.

HARDY, R.M., Cropwell Bishop, nr. Ratcliffe-on-Trent, Notts.

HARMSWORTH, A., "Dowend," Chatsworth Rd., Worthing, Sussex.

HARNESS, H., 66 Barnby Gate, Newark, Notts.

HARRIS, S.A., Lower Herne, Herne, Kent.

HARRIS, T., 5 Baranden St., Notting Hill, London.

HARRISON, A.E., 123 Philip St., Patricroft, Manchester.

HARRISON, F.W., 18 Seeley Rd., Lenton Sands, Notts.

HARRY, R.R., 110 Nolton St., Bridgend, Glam.

HART, E., 32 Church St., Sutton-in-Ashfield, Notts.

HART, J., 5 Arundel Drive, Mansfield, Notts.

HARTILL, E., Smyth Cottage, Maidstone, Kent.

HAYES, H., Belle Eau Park Farm, Kirklington, Notts.

HAYES, J.C., Belle Eau Park Farm, Kirklington, Notts.

HAYMAN, J.T., Foresters Arms, High St., Reynsham, Bristol.

HAYWARD, J. (Saddler), 33 Princess Rd., Lower Broughton, Manchester.

HEARN, G., 3 Westfield Rd., Edinburgh.

HEATHCOTE, E., 16 Cromwell Rd., Nottingham (killed at Tahta).

HEMMINGWAY, F., 21 High St., Batley Carr, Batley, Yorks.

HENDERSON, A., The Smithy, Carnoustie, Scotland.

HENSON, T., 47 Chaplain St., Lincoln.

HERRINGTON, R., South Carlton, nr. Worksop, Notts.

HESKETH, E., Newton Green, Alfreton, Derbyshire.

HESLOP, W., 53 Heath St., Stepney, E.

HICKING, J.S., Chatham House, Munday St., Henor, Derby.

HOLBOROW, J., Didmarton, Badminton, Glos.

HOLDER, J., 40 Braydon Rd., Clapton, N.

HOLLINGWORTH, T., 74 Westfield Rd., Caversham, nr. Reading.

HOODLESS, J., Bridgend, Dalston.

HORSTEAD, H., 23 Winterton Rd., Sunthorpe, Lincs.

HOWLETT, J., 119 Brookdale Rd., Catford, S.E.

HUDSON, G.H., 5 Blackfriar St., Stamford.

HUDSON, L., 84 Low St., Keighley, Yorks.

HUDSON, ——, Westgate Rd. Fire Station, Newcastle-on-Tyne.

HUGGETT, G., 19 Cornwall Rd., Brixton, S.W.

HUNT, B., 140 Armagh Rd., Bow, E.

HUNT, E., 5 Bartholomew Cottages, Gillingham, Kent.

HUNT, J., 68 St. Paul's Terrace, Holgate Rd., York.

HUNT, S.F.R., Box 53 P.O., Prince George, British Columbia.

HUTCHINS, G. (Saddle Cpl.), Orchard Lane, Alton, Hants.

HYDE, E.W., 141 Glyn Rd., London, N.E.

INGRAM, F.A., 85 Broad St., Tottenham, London, N.

INKLEY, E.A., 96 St. Anne's Well Rd., Nottingham.

IRVINE, R.J., 140 Roebank St., Dennistoun, Glasgow.

JACQUES, A., 3 Halls Cottages, Stapleford, Notts.

JACQUES, J., " " "

JAMES, C.F., 34 Newcastle Hill, Bridgend, Glam.

JARVIS, E., 75 Lyndhurst Rd., Sneinton Dale, Nottingham.

JARVIS, W.B., 70 Eldon St., Greenock, Scotland.

JENKINS, E., West Farm, Llantwith Major, Cardiff.

JOHNSTON, J., 52 Hyde Park St., Anderston, Glasgow (died 15-10-18, Damascus).

JOHNSTON, R., Charleston-by-Glamis, Forfar.

JOYNCE, C.

KAVANAH, R., 14 Park Grove Rd., Leytonstone, Essex.

KEARN, G., Dean Farm, Willey Broseley, Salop.

KEMP, A., 13 Baumont St., Sneinton, Notts.

KEMSLEY, J., Breadgar, nr. Sittingbourne, Kent.
KENNY, R., Newton-on-Ouse, nr. York.
KENT. S.C., 28 Scaresdale St., Carr Vale, Bolsover, Derbyshire.
KITE, W.J., Witney Rd., Finstock, Charlbury, Oxon.
KNIGHT, L.J., Hanescombe, nr. Brookthorpe, Gloucester.
KNOTT, E., Lord St., Mansfield, Notts.
LAKE, J., 8 King St., Tibshelf, nr. Alfreton, Derby.
LAMBDEN, E.J., Ivy Bridge, Bourne End, Bucks.
LAMBIE, J., 21 Shamrock St., New City Rd., Glasgow.
LAND, F., Lynton Rd., Porlock, Somerset.
LARCOMBE, W., Chardstock, Chard, Somerset.
LAURIE, W., 27 Margaret St., Hixbourne, Birmingham.
LEAFE, F.F., 5 Birkland Avenue, Peel St., Nottingham (killed Tel el Quelfi).
LEE, P., 7 Strawberry Terrace, Newtown, Retford, Notts.
LEEDALE, J.B., Victoria House, Bourne, Lincs.
LESLIE, C., 145 Princess St., Dundee.
LEVERTON, C., Abbott St., Asworth, Notts.
LINES, A.J., 66 Church St., Oldbury, Staffs.
LOWE, W.H., Cuckney, Mansfield, Notts.
LOY, P.A., "St. Malo," Midmay Rd , Romford, Essex.
LUMB, P.J., 2 Upper Oxford St., Doncaster.
MACINTOSH, A., 157 Ewart Rd., Forest Fields, Nottingham.
MACKENZIE, W., The Cottage, Balfour Place, Kirkcaldy.
MANN, J., Seafield St., Cullen, Banffshire.
MAPLETOFT, L., The Cottage, Great Gonerby, Grantham.
MARRIOTT, J., 63 Nottingham Rd., Stapleford, Notts.
MARSHALL, F., 19 Lawrence St., York.
MARSHALL, J.L., 257 Sherwood St., Nottingham.
MATHEWS, W.H., 39 Eperns Rd. Fulham, S.W.
MATTOCKS, W.J., 122 Lower Addiscombe Rd., East Croydon, Surrey.
MCDONALD, M., Sabbell Village, Carradale, Argyleshire.
MCLELLAN, E.R., 110 Leddard Rd., Langside, Glasgow.
MCLENNAN, J., 80 Cudrethal Rd., Inverness.
MELLOWS, S., 12 Whyburn St., Hucknall, Nott. (died).
MILES, A.H., 25 Rutland St., Pimlico, S.W.
MILES, A.H. (Wheeler), 49 Greet Rd., Brentford, Middlesex.
MILLAN, T., West Bank Place, Falkirk, Scotland.
MILNTHORPE, H., 28 South Parade, Doncaster.
MITCHELL, J.P., 99 Whitfield St., Fitzroy Square, London.
MORRIS, S., 64 Darrel Rd., Retford, Notts.
MOYES, A.E., 6 West Lane, Sittingbourne, Kent.
MURRAY, J.J., Porters Well, Uddingston, Lanark.
MUSSON, J., 176 Foxhill Rd., Carlton, Notts. (killed in action, Damascus, 30-9-18).
NIX, T.V., Cherry House, Red Hill Rd., Arnold, Notts.
OLDHAM, J.J., Carleton-on-Trent, Newark.
OLIVANT, G., Nettleham Lodge, Nr. Lincoln.

ORDISH, E.A., 17 Sketchley St., Bluebell Hill, Nottingham.
OSBORNE, A.W., 32 New St., Chelmsford, Essex.
PAMPLING, W., 193 Newmarket Rd., Cambridge (died).
PARKIN, F.W., The Lodge, Scrooby, Bawtry, Yorks.
PARKIN, S., 31 Kilbourne St., Nottingham.
PATTERSON, W., Monaltrie Rd., Ballater.
PEACH, L., Eccleston, Amersham, Bucks.
PEARSON, H., 32 Hope St., Brampton, Chesterfield.
PEARSON, T., 20 Bloomsgrove St., Radford, Notts.
PEEL, A., Newport, Lincoln.
PERRY, A., Sturtingale Cottage, Rush Hill, Bath.
PHILLIPS, C., 29 Thorn St., Derby.
PITTS, J., 10 South Parade, Bath.
PRICE, E., The Turfs, Norton Canes, Camrock, Staffs.
PRICE, M., Quinton, Pennfields, Wolverhampton.
PRICE, W.A.C.H., 8 Camden Rd., Stamford.
PRITCHARD, S., Rosemount, Ponkey, Wrexham.
QUESTED, R., Park Gate Farm, Elham, nr. Canterbury, Kent.
RATCLIFFE, J., 17 Old Paradise St., Lambeth, S.E.
REED, H., 33 Church Terrace, Tower Rd., Erith.
REEKMANS, W. (Saddler), 20 Ducie St., Brixton, S.W.
RICHMOND, E.J., Moorgate Hill, Retford, Notts.
RIDGWAY, A., "Goat's Head," Lillingstone, Daysell, Bucks.
RILEY, E.A., 31 Weston St., Nechells, Birmingham (taken prisoner 1-11-17, supposed wounded, not since heard of, presumed dead by W.O.).
RIPPIN, F., 10 King's Head Place, Market Harboro', Leics.
ROBERTS, W., 82 Brunswick St., The Mount, York.
ROBERTSON, A., 192 New City Rd., Glasgow.
ROBINSON, H. (Signaller), 120 Nottingham Rd., Mansfield, Notts.
RUARK, A.C., 8 Wanlip Rd., Plaistow, E.
RUSH, E., Co-Operative Yard, Worksop, Notts.
SAVORY, S.W., St. Peter's Rd., Cleethorpes, Lincs.
SCOTT, W., 20 Thames St., Retford, Notts.
SEAMAN, C.W., 60 Lee St., Holderness Rd., Hull.
SEARS (S/Smith), 9 Back Cottages, Commercial Rd., Bullwell, Notts.
SHARPE, C.A., 51 Gedling Rd., Carlton, Notts.
SHARPE, W.F., 119 Ryland Rd., Edgbaston, Birmingham.
SHEPHERD, J., 37 Plantation St., Wallsend-on-Tyne.
SHERRATT, C., 4 Crown Terrace, Basford, Notts.
SHORT, P.C., North Aston, nr. Deddington, Oxon.
SIDDALL, J.C., 11 Sedd St., Ratcliffe, nr. Manchester.
SINCLAIR, J., 42 Stewart Terrace, Edinburgh.
SISSON, A., 41 Hempshill Lane, Bulwell, Notts.
SISSONS, E., 3 Honey Place, Main St., Bulwell, Notts.
SLEIGHTHOLME, A., Atworth, Melksham, Wilts.
SMITH, C., Kneeton Rd., East Bridgford, Notts.
SMITH, C.W., 37 Bishopbridge Rd., Norwich.

SMITH, E.C., 1 Fern Cottages, St. Osyth Rd., Clacton-on-Sea.

SMITH, H., 4 Dulwich Rd., Radford, Notts.

SMITH, W., 94 Blackstone St., Nottingham.

SMITH, W.J., The Barracks, Westcott, nr. Dorking, Surrey.

SOPER, W., 36 Brandon Buildings, Clifton, Bristol.

SOUTHEY, G.E., 46 Brownlow Rd., Putney, S.W.

SPENCER, F., 80 Laughton Rd., Dennington, nr. Rotherham.

SPENCER, G., 37 Ortzen St., Radford, Notts.

SPENCER, G., 37 Padiham Rd., Burnley, Lancs. (died).

SPINKS, W.K., West End, Ely, Cambs.

SPRATT, B., 13 Methley St., Meadow Rd., Leeds.

SPRINGETT, A.J., Avon's Dale, Colchester.

STANILAND, A., 6 Howard Rd., Mansfield, Notts. (killed Damascus).

STANLEY, A.B. (Signaller), 16 New Rd., Ridgwood, Uckfield, Sussex.

STAPLETON, H., Bulcot Lodge Farm, Burton Joyce, Notts.

STRANKS, T.H., 43 Quarry St., Milverton, Leamington.

STRAW, A., 2 Tennyson Terrace, Hawksley Rd., Nottingham.

STROSS, G., 40 Brighton Rd., Birkdale, Southport.

TALBOTT, F.C., 134 Church Square, Newport, Salop.

TANNER, H.G., Police Station, Amesbury, Wilts.

TAYLOR, E.E., "Brim Cottage," Griffiths Crossing, Carnarvon.

TEGGIN, H., "The Pentre," St. Martins, Oswestry, Salop.

THOMAS, J.E., Pillford, Milford Haven.

THOMPSON, A., Whitwell, Mansfield, Notts.

THOMPSON, A.M., Greenhead Gate, Lanark.

THOMPSON, D.J., 61 Henderson St., Glasgow.

THORNHILL, H., 48 Park Rd., Lenton, Nottingham.

THORPE, C., 18 Gordon Hill, Enfield, Middx.

TIVEY, A., 5 Gedling Rd., Carlton, Notts.

TOINTON, J., Elmsford House, Spalding, Lincs.

TOLHURST, W.G., 9 Marden Lane, London.

TOOKE, R., "Horseshoes," Scottow, Norwich.

TOOLEY, H.A.

TRIPP, S.H., 116 Nag's Head Hill, St. George, Bristol.

TUBBS, H.C., 7 Warwick Villas, Homerton, N.E.

TURNBULL, J., 16 Lothian St., Hawick.

TURNER, G.

TURNER, W.E., "The Admiral Napier," Weedington Rd., Kentish Town, N.W.

TYLER, B.H. School House, Ironville, Derby.

VAUGHAN, T.G., Rock House, nr. Bewley, Worcester.

VEITCH, J. (S/Smith), 86 Scott St., Galashiels, Scotland.

WALKER, A., 150 Moorbottom Rd., Crosland Moor, Huddersfield.

WALLACE, G., 828 Argyle St., Glasgow.

WALPOLE, A.N., Anthills Farm, Redhall, Harleston, Norfolk.

WALSHAW, L.J., 56 Cannon St., Belgrave, Leicester.

WANSTALL, P.N.

WARD, B.V., "Sankta Koro,"Vallance Rd., Muswell Hill, N.
WATERSON, A., 16 North Junction St., Leith, Scotland.
WATSON, B.E., Rose Cottage, Girton, Cambridge.
WATSON, J., 2 Lightfoot Buildings, Cinque Ports St., Rye, Sussex.
WATTS, C.P., 7 Brown's Rd., Plaistow, E.
WEATHERLEY, E.J., 120 Lovatt St., Grimsby.
WEBB, C.J., 21 Lower Addiscombe Rd., Croydon, Surrey.
WEIGHILL, A., 70 Oxford St., Barnsley.
WHITBY, J., 26 Lower Brook St., Long Eaton, Notts.
WHITE, C.F., 21 Pelham St., Brighton, Sussex.
WHITE, S., Frilsham, Yattendon, Newbury, Berks.
WHITLOCK, G.H., 44 Bushy Park, Tottendown, Bristol.
WICK, S., 13 Golden Dog's Lane, Norwich.
WILBRAHAM, ——, Barton, Malpas, Cheshire.
WILLIAMS, G., Collets Green, Porwick, Worcester.
WILSON, A., 21 Chisholm Rd., Croydon, Surrey.
WINFIELD, R.J., Checkendon, nr. Reading, Oxon.
WOOD, F., 6 Barfields, Bletchingley, Surrey.
WORTHINGTON, J.W., 41 The Hill, Kirby-in-Ashfield.
WRIGHT, T., "Ivy House," Aixley, Corringham Gainsboro', Lincs.
WROOT, B., High St., Misterton, Notts.

Roll of Honour

As a result of the circular letter dated 3-6-20, referred to on page 172, the following names have been received of those Members of the 20th Machine-Gun Squadron who have made the *supreme sacrifice* in their Country's service:

MAJOR L.F. ST. JOHN DAVIES, M.C\.

LIEUT. H A. PRICE, M.C.

SERGT. W.H. MORDEN

LCE. CORPL. F. CARR

LCE. CORPL. A. MARRIOTT

PRIVATE G. BOAK

PRIVATE B. CAPEL

PRIVATE P. CHANTRY

PRIVATE H.C. GOLDIE

PRIVATE E. HEATHCOTE

PRIVATE J. JOHNSTON

PRIVATE F.F. LEAFE

PRIVATE S. MELLOWS

PRIVATE J. MUSSON

PRIVATE W. PAMPLING

PRIVATE E.A. RILEY

PRIVATE G. SPENCER

PRIVATE A. STANILAND(

N.B.—The above, it is feared, does not include all the names in spite of every effort that has been made to obtain a complete list.

ALSO FROM LEONAUR

AVAILABLE IN SOFTCOVER OR HARDCOVER WITH DUST JACKET

SEPOYS, SIEGE & STORM *by Charles John Griffiths*—The Experiences of a young officer of H.M.'s 61st Regiment at Ferozepore, Delhi ridge and at the fall of Delhi during the Indian mutiny 1857.

CAMPAIGNING IN ZULULAND *by W. E. Montague*—Experiences on campaign during the Zulu war of 1879 with the 94th Regiment.

THE STORY OF THE GUIDES *by G. J. Younghusband*—The Exploits of the Soldiers of the famous Indian Army Regiment from the northwest frontier 1847 - 1900..

ZULU: 1879 *by D.C.F. Moodie & the Leonaur Editors*—The Anglo-Zulu War of 1879 from contemporary sources: First Hand Accounts, Interviews, Dispatches, Official Documents & Newspaper Reports.

THE RECOLLECTIONS OF SKINNER OF SKINNER'S HORSE *by James Skinner*—James Skinner and his 'Yellow Boys' Irregular cavalry in the wars of India between the British, Mahratta, Rajput, Mogul, Sikh & Pindarree Forces.

TOMMY ATKINS' WAR STORIES 14 FIRST HAND ACCOUNTS—Fourteen first hand accounts from the ranks of the British Army during Queen Victoria's Empire Original & True Battle Stories Recollections of the Indian Mutiny With the 49th in the Crimea With the Guards in Egypt The Charge of the Six Hundred With Wolseley in Ashanti Alma, Inkermann and Magdala With the Gunners at Tel-el-Kebir Russian Guns and Indian Rebels Rough Work in the Crimea In the Maori Rising Facing the Zulus From Sebastopol to Lucknow Sent to Save Gordon On the March to Chitral Tommy by Rudyard Kipling

CHASSEUR OF 1914 *by Marcel Dupont*—Experiences of the twilight of the French Light Cavalry by a young officer during the early battles of the great war in Europe.

TROOP HORSE & TRENCH *by R. A. Lloyd*—The experiences of a British Lifeguardsman of the household cavalry fighting on the western front during the First World War 1914-18.

THE EAST AFRICAN MOUNTED RIFLES *by C. J. Wilson*—Experiences of the campaign in the East African bush during the First World War.

THE FIGHTING CAMELIERS *by Frank Reid*—The exploits of the Imperial Camel Corps in the desert and Palestine campaigns of the First World War.